www.layout

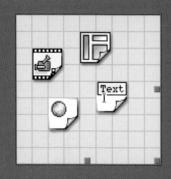

www.layout

JERRY GLENWRIGHT

SERIES CONSULTANT
ALASTAIR CAMPBELL

WATSON-GUPTILL
PUBLICATIONS
New York

First published in the
United States in 2001 by
Watson-Guptill
Publications,
a division of BPI
Communications, Inc.,
770 Broadway,
New York, NY 10003

Library of Congress
Catalog Card Number:
00-111832

ISBN 0-8230-5858-1

This book was conceived,
designed and produced
by The Ilex Press Limited
The Barn, College Farm
1 West End, Whittlesford
Cambridge CB2 4LX
England
Sales Office:
The Old Candlemakers
West Street, Lewes
East Sussex BN7 2NZ
England

Art Director:
Alastair Campbell
Managing Editor:
Kim Yarwood
Editor:
Corinne Orde
Indexer:
Mary Orchard
Designer:
Angela Neal
Additional material:
Trevor Bounford

Originated and printed in
China by Hong Kong
Graphic, Hong Kong

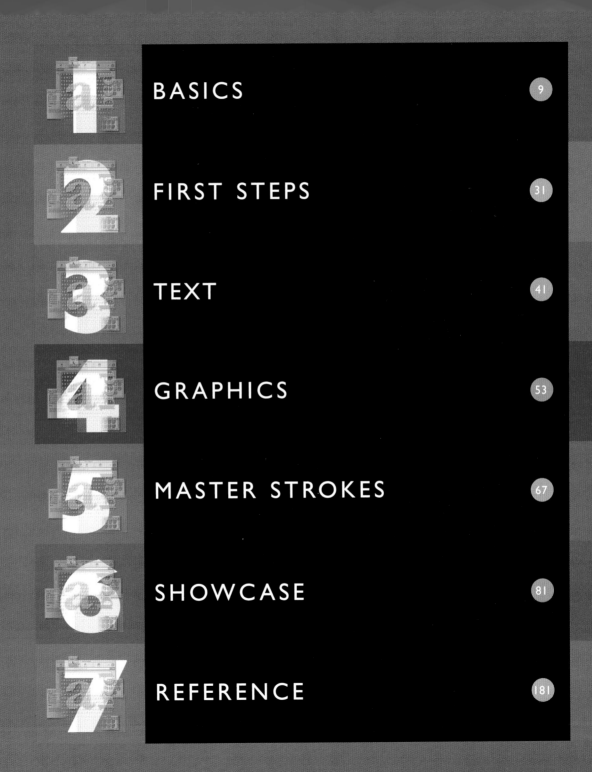

INTRODUCTION

t's young, it's vibrant, it's brash, bright, and a design rule-breaker like no other medium you've ever worked with. The Internet is the coolest place to be if you're a graphic designer brimming over with groundbreaking ideas. But it's also a new and strange place for designers who previously have worked with "traditional" tools such as an Apple Macintosh computer and QuarkXPress, or even—dare we say it!—paper, galleys of typeset text, a Rotring, Spray Mount, and a scalpel.

For starters, the vast majority of machines attached to the Internet are PCs (or, even more esoteric, "Unix boxes"), and even if they're running the Mac-like Windows interface (or X-Windows in the case of Unix machines), using and designing for them can be a very different experience indeed. Designs published on the World Wide Web (or "WWW," "W3," or "Web") exist only as bits and bytes inside a computer.

The Web is a virtual world—you can experience it, but you can't touch it. Pictures, sounds, animations, video, and all the other snazzy effects that you enjoy while surfing are the visible and aural end result of some pretty obscure computer code winding its digital way between computers over the interconnected network of computer networks (hence "inter-net") that is the Internet.

Jerry Glenwright

Norwich, England

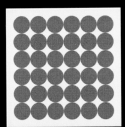 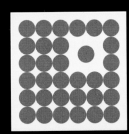 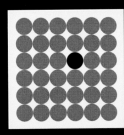 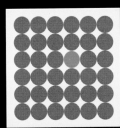 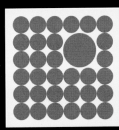

Whatever the elements of a page layout, its success—both functionally and aesthetically—depends entirely on emphasis. Disparate elements with equal emphasis can look dull and confusing.

You can achieve maximum effect with minimum modification: simply rearranging the elements will give emphasis to one just by creating space.

Equally, you can give effective emphasis to textual elements— even HTML—simply by emboldening a character, word, or phrase.

You can also use color effectively by limiting its use to only those elements that require it. Emphasis is not lost— and can indeed be stressed—by modifying both weight *and* color.

Probably the most common approach to emphasising elements on Web pages is to increase their size. While this can be effective when applied with discretion, it's all too easy to fall into the trap of overkill—the more elements you enlarge, the more you reduce emphasis.

8

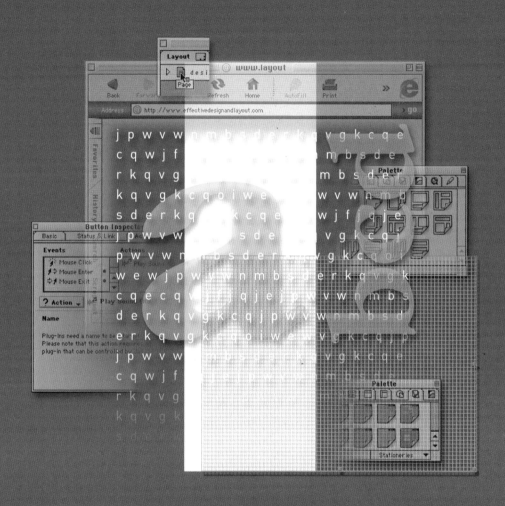

WHAT IS LAYOUT?

VizAbility™ is a modular "visual thinking kit", designed to help you discover, explore and improve your natural visual abilities. Experience VizAbility™, and change the way you see the world.

esign is the functional realization of what would otherwise be fine art. Like an artist, a designer strives to create something that arouses the aesthetical sense. For the artist the creative process ends there and the interpretation of the work lies with those who experience it—that's why arguments rage (and have always raged) about what constitutes art. The only truth is that there is no clear definition other than that art's "function" is simply to be, to exist—an upside-down urinal and a sixteenth–century female with an enigmatic smile.

No such conflict exists in design. Form is combined with functionality to create something which is at once pretty and purposeful. A product brochure works only if

10

You're my new favorite client

MetaWho?   Projects   Clients   MetaCulture   Jobs

MetaDesign

MetaDesign is an international design firm specializing in identity, branding, interaction design and information design. Our clients bring us a wide variety of projects that are diverse in scope, timing, and complexity.

⇢ **Identity & Branding**

Creating a compelling brand in today's digital economy requires a different approach and we have a lot of thoughts on how the playing field has changed. Browse through some of our recent identity projects to see more about our approach.

⇢ **Interaction Design**

We bring a systems-thinking approach to the creation of Web sites, product interfaces, and even the design of physical spaces.

1 | 2 | 3

Online design is as good as that found in other forms, but far more bad design is found in the virtual world than in the real world. Good designs include Vizability **www.vizability.com**, with its gallery-like front page; MetaDesign **www.metadesign.com**, with its hip design; and DKNY's **www.dkny.com** minimalist offering.

DKNY

2

3

4

Vizability again, with an interesting way of saying "Don't steal our fonts." The layout is very simple but ultimately memorable.

5

A contemporary color scheme allied with strong sans serif type and clean icons give MetaDesign's site a powerful presence.

it imparts the information essential to making a purchase—however beautifully designed the brochure. Conversely, a brochure crammed with useful information but which is ugly won't attract buyers. Books and magazines must be pleasing and legible, chocolate wrappers mouthwatering and able to protect the chocolate within, and Web sites amazing, anarchic, animated, beautiful, compatible, fast, and usable.

From the early "logo and a few pics" affairs, commercial Web sites have evolved into living, breathing outlets for businesses eager to promote their products and services but which also want to make a Web presence pay. The dot.com culture is becoming broadly acceptable to an otherwise largely network-illiterate user group. It is first-class Web designers who are driving forward that acceptance by creating Web sites that are accessible,

beautiful, and usable—Web sites that draw in visitors and enable them to navigate what a site has to offer.

Web layout should, in theory, be just like any other kind: the baseline for what constitutes a "good" design applies equally to cyberspace. What the Web offers over traditional publishing is a virtual world's worth of glorious gadgets for sound and animation. Web layout effects are cheap and cheerful and available to anyone with the desire to learn. Some of the better sites are showcased later in this book. Look at them and try to absorb the quintessential qualities that make them stand out over the millions of others on the World Wide Web competing for visitors. Go to the sites, open them with a Web-authoring tool, and see what it is that makes these sites tick. Take the best of what they offer and discard the rest, but above all have fun!

A BIT OF HISTORY

Web pages have almost no limits size-wise. What you see on screen is an endlessly scrolling sheet of virtual paper with a horizontal width limited only by the resolution of the monitor you're working with (and that of the monitors of those who will ultimately view your Web pages). Typically, a Web page will be set to display 800 by 600 pixels, but there are many variations.

It's your task as a designer to impose limits on this otherwise limitless cyberspace, limits that will ensure high-quality design yet make the most of the many novel features the new medium offers.

You do this by using a special Web programming language or a software package that obviates the need for programming skills and enables you to directly manipulate text and graphics.

Web code is called "HyperText Markup Language," or HTML for short, and it's the reason why the Web part of the Internet came about in the first place. Initially, the Internet was a text-only interchange. Users sent each other e-mails and text files and accessed primitive on-line bulletin boards called newsgroups (though there's precious little actual "news"). Back then, the Internet was largely restricted to the military and academics, neither particularly noted for their flair or imagination.

Things continued in this way for a number of years until Tim Berners-Lee, a programmer at CERN (Conseil Européen pour la Recherche Nucléaire, the European Laboratory for Particle Physics) in Switzerland, decided that it might be a good idea to link the many pieces of information scattered around the Internet in such a way that all of it would become cross-referenced—you might be reading about Wiltshire crop circles and then, by clicking on a link embedded in the text, cause a document to appear detailing how to create your own circles.

Berners-Lee described his notion as a "world wide web of random associations between arbitrary pieces of information." He developed a program to make

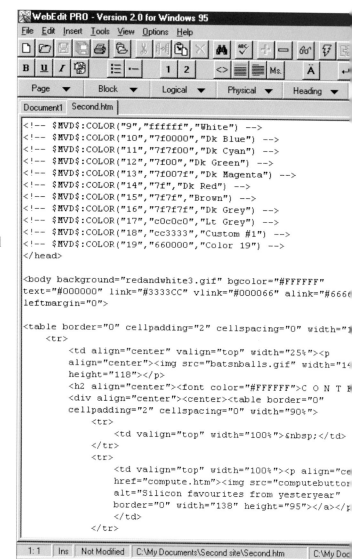

and navigate these associations (the forerunner of the browser) and called it "Enquire," after the popular Victorian book *Enquire Within Upon Everything*—still in print in the 1970s—which offered helpful hints on unrelated subjects to householders. The Enquire program used "hypertext links" (or "hyperlinks") between information. That was 1980.

Though an excellent and viable idea, few others saw its potential. And so it languished for a decade until 1992, when Marc Andreessen, a postgraduate student at

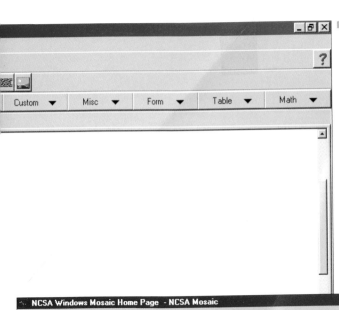

Custom ▼	Misc ▼	Form ▼	Table ▼	Math ▼

1
HTML is a text-tagging system, not a computer programming language. The basic code is seeded with tiny computer programs, however, that bring Web pages alive.

2
Mosaic was the world's first graphical Web browser and it's still available today as a free download, albeit in much improved form.

13

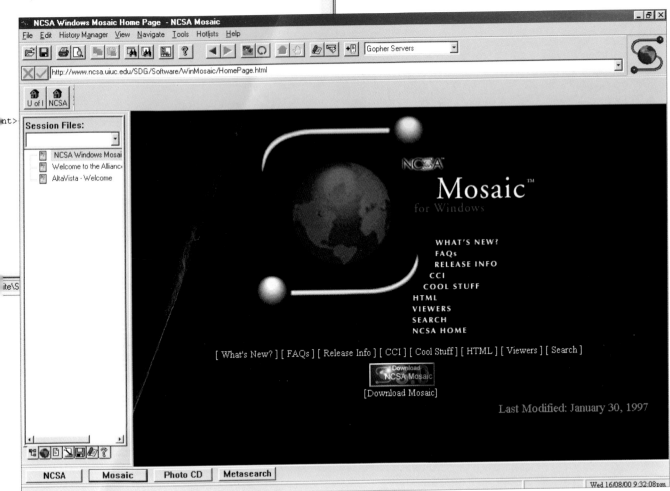

NCSA Windows Mosaic Home Page - NCSA Mosaic

File   Edit   History Manager   View   Navigate   Tools   Hotlists   Help

Gopher Servers

http://www.ncsa.uiuc.edu/SDG/Software/WinMosaic/HomePage.html

U of I   NCSA

Session Files:

NCSA Windows Mosai
Welcome to the Allianc
AltaVista - Welcome

NCSA
Mosaic™
for Windows

WHAT'S NEW?
FAQs
RELEASE INFO
CCI
COOL STUFF
HTML
VIEWERS
SEARCH
NCSA HOME

[What's New?] [FAQs] [Release Info] [CCI] [Cool Stuff] [HTML] [Viewers] [Search]

Download
NCSA Mosaic
[Download Mosaic]

Last Modified: January 30, 1997

NCSA   Mosaic   Photo CD   Metasearch

Wed 16/08/00 9:32:08pm

A BIT OF HISTORY (CONTINUED)

the University of Illinois at Urbana-Champaign, happened upon Tim Berners-Lee's World Wide Web and was immediately captivated. However, Andreessen instantly recognized its one real shortcoming: the lack of a Web browser with a graphical interface. He determined to write one. The result was a browser with a point-and-click interface, which he called "Mosaic for X" (X being the graphical user interface (GUI) front-end used on computers running the Unix and Linux operating systems).

Andreessen converted his GUI-based Mosaic browser to work on the PC and Apple Macintosh, and then made it available free for download by anyone on the Internet. Within a year there were a million users worldwide. The rest, as they say, is history.

So Web pages (or "sites" or whatever you like to call them) are created with HTML. This is translated in real time (i.e. as you watch) by a browser such as Microsoft's Explorer or Netscape's Navigator into the familiar graphical format of a Web page.

It should be noted that HTML is not a computer programming language in itself. HTML is a system of tagging text to enable it to be displayed in styles such as bold, italic, and so on. However, since the Web also features snazzy effects such as animation, sounds, and live video, the bland HTML is seeded with miniature computer programs known as "applets." These are written using one of several cut-down computer languages, such as Java, JavaScript, VBscript, and so on. Taken altogether, it's reasonable to describe the process of creating Web pages in this way as programming.

Programming language? Real-time translations? Fortunately for designers, the need to learn to program has—almost—passed. Software companies such as Adobe and Microsoft have been quick to exploit the need for software packages that enable designers to

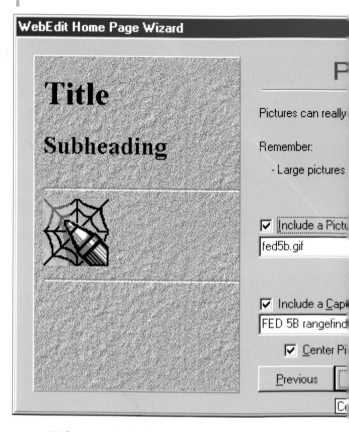

create Web pages in the same way that desktop publishing software (QuarkXPress et. al) enables them to create printed materials.

And "Web-authoring software," as it is known, works in much the same way as DTP software. You import text and graphics onto "pages," manipulating them and then viewing them just as they would appear on screen via the Internet.

Web-authoring software was at first crude, requiring designers to tinker with HTML in order to achieve anything more than "a picture, some text" layouts. Gradually, however, the various packages have evolved into useful tools that almost entirely remove the need for programming. We'll take a closer look at HTML code and Web-authoring software later in this chapter.

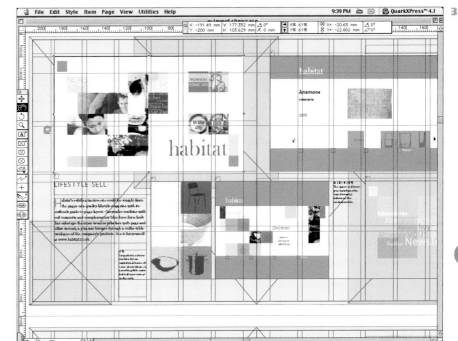

1 | 2
Web-authoring
software was at first
crude, and designers
making the transition
from QuarkXPress
found the new
concepts difficult
to grasp.

3
Many Web designers
prefer to manipulate
HTML directly—an
onerous task but one
that gives extreme
power over every
aspect of Web–page
layout. Using Web-
authoring software
can be like designing
via remote control…

15

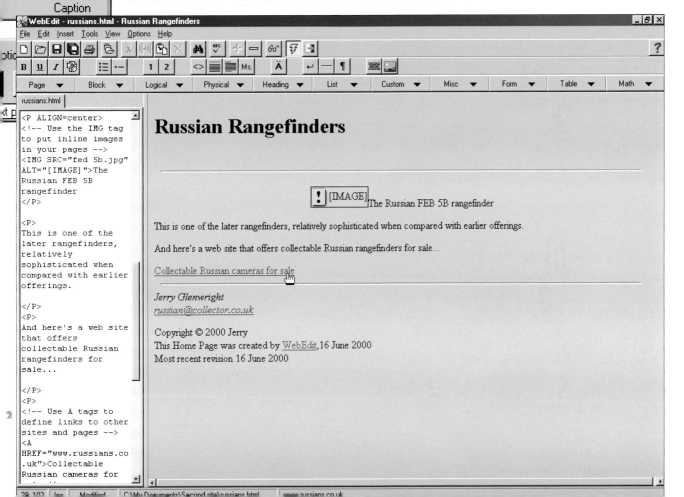

Russian Rangefinders

[IMAGE] The Russian FEB 5B rangefinder

This is one of the later rangefinders, relatively sophisticated when compared with earlier offerings.

And here's a web site that offers collectable Russian rangefinders for sale…

Collectable Russian cameras for sale

Jerry Glenwright
russian@collector.co.uk

Copyright © 2000 Jerry
This Home Page was created by WebEdit, 16 June 2000
Most recent revision 16 June 2000

```
<P ALIGN=center>
<!-- Use the IMG tag
to put inline images
in your pages -->
<IMG SRC="fed 5b.jpg"
ALT="[IMAGE]">The
Russian FEB 5B
rangefinder
</P>

<P>
This is one of the
later rangefinders,
relatively
sophisticated when
compared with earlier
offerings.

</P>
<P>
And here's a web site
that offers
collectable Russian
rangefinders for
sale...

</P>
<P>
<!-- Use A tags to
define links to other
sites and pages -->
<A
HREF="www.russians.co
.uk">Collectable
Russian cameras for
```

HOW A WEB SITE IS ORGANIZED

A Web site is the visual (and sometimes aural) representation of what would otherwise be a drab collection of text files and the directories that contain them. HTML documents include the essential instructions for publishing your page in cyberspace, and these documents are almost always accompanied by support files such as illustrations, buttons, animations (in the form of JPGs and GIFs), sounds, and video clips.

Even a modest personal home page will generate a surprising number of these files, and anything more complicated—such as a business-oriented site featuring linked content pages—will account for megabytes of the stuff.

Poor organization and planning at the start will result in a confusing site that is difficult to maintain properly—and so you'll stop bothering, with the inevitable result that people will stop visiting. There's little more off-putting on the Web than arriving at an obviously out-of-date site which hasn't seen the guiding hand of its author in ages.

Key to high-quality presentation is sensible organization, and it's a factor which you must get right at the outset—particularly if you think the site will evolve and grow (as most do). So, long before settling down at the keyboard, get a pad of paper and a pencil and write out the aims of the site, its proposed audience, structure, and likely content. This will enable you to effectively plan its organization, and the result could be a site with a hit counter that goes into meltdown!

Begin by deciding just what it is you want to say, and understand that your message will be infinitely more palatable if you wrap it up in something useful. The really outstanding Web sites give visitors something more than what the Web master smugly assumes is a unique visual extravaganza. Useful or rare information, a snippet of free software, or a how-to guide—whatever your site is about—offers visitors something to take

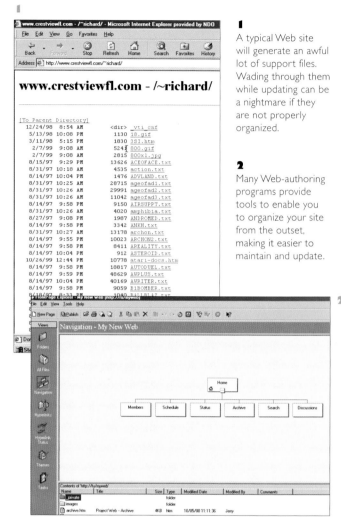

1
A typical Web site will generate an awful lot of support files. Wading through them while updating can be a nightmare if they are not properly organized.

2
Many Web-authoring programs provide tools to enable you to organize your site from the outset, making it easier to maintain and update.

away and you'll score a hit. Being added to the visitor's all-important bookmarks list is what you're aiming to achieve, and adding value is the way to achieve it.

Having decided on your message, determine how to present it. The accepted method is to open a site with a home ("index" or "doorway") page, which features little more than a title and tools to navigate through the rest of the site. At this stage you might decide that frames (see Chapter 5) would be a good way to delineate the various site areas and to separate intermediate and

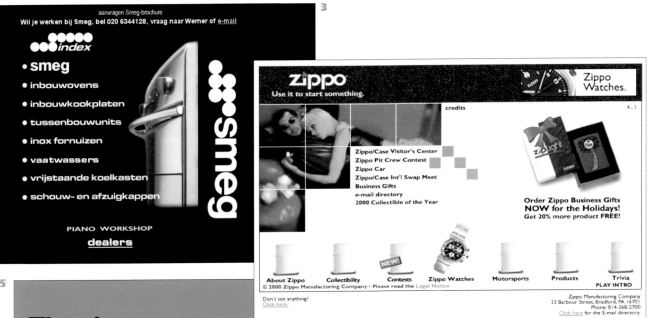

3
Try to make an index page that doesn't have to be scrolled either vertically or horizontally. An attractive and complete master with bite-sized chunks of information and links to subpages has more drawing power. Smeg's **www.smeg.nl** very simple index page takes us where we need to go without bafflement, while a jumble of data would take an age to download and turn visitors away.

4 | 5
Avoid the temptation to put too much on a single page in a bid for attention. Zippo **www.zippo.com** has managed to include a lot with some slick animations. The layout is busy, but not crammed. Thumb **www.thumb.co.uk** takes the opposite approach and provides "teasers," which tempt visitors into clicking further into the site, navigating its pages, and seeing what they have to offer.

content pages. You might go for a combination of both types of page or set up distinct sites for each so that the visitor can choose.

Although it is possible to place everything needed for the site into one directory on your server, a much better idea is to break up the available space—say, 20 megabytes—into a master directory and subdirectories, each devoted to the content of one page. The data will be easier to manage and maintain, and you can put a page up or take it down simply by removing its HTML file. Of course, you could do this even if all the elements of your site were lumped together in a single directory, but wading through to find what you wanted would be a tedious process.

HTML AND ITS DERIVATIVES

Though it might look horrifyingly complex to non-programmers, HTML is actually a comparatively simple system of "tags" that specify type styles and sizes, the location of graphics, and all the other information required to construct a Web page. However, the language is extremely verbose—even the simplest pages require many lines of code, which means that modifying existing pages is at best time-consuming, as you wade through masses of code looking for the lines you want to change.

What's more, Web pages created solely from HTML would be exceedingly boring, so otherwise plain-text HTML documents sport embedded mini-computer programs known as "applets," which provide the whizzy effects, such as animations, hit counters, rollover buttons, and the like, seen on most Web pages.

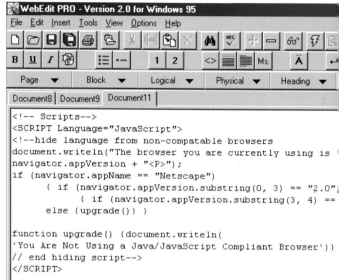

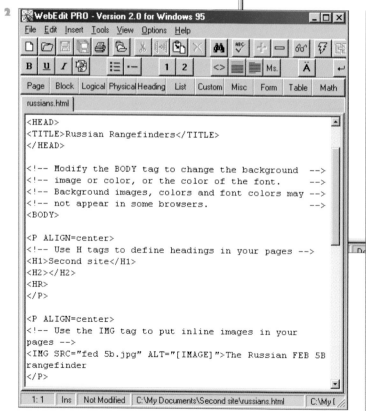

1 | 2
HTML provides the building blocks from which Web pages are constructed. But the system of text tags is extremely verbose.

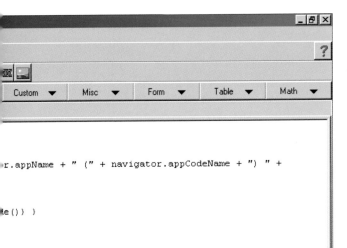

```
r.appName + " (" + navigator.appCodeName + ") " +

e()} }
```

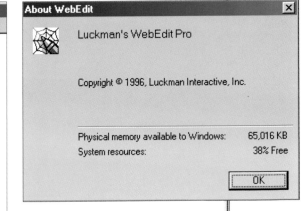

```
Sense</TH>

 select</TD>

 printer</TD></TR>
to EPROM</TD></TR>
to EPROM</TD>

></TR>
to EPROM</TD>

></TR>
to EPROM</TD>

></TR>
to EPROM</TD>

></TR>
to EPROM</TD>

></TR>
to EPROM</TD>

></TR>
om EPROM</TD>

</TD></TR>
om EPROM</TD>

</TD></TR>
om EPROM</TD>

</TD></TR>
om EPROM</TD>

</TD></TR>
```

3
Try typing in that stuff and see how many mistakes you make! This is the HTML code to make a tabbed table.

4
WebEdit Pro is one of the better HTML editing suites and provides many features to make the manipulation of HTML a little easier.

 19

The applets are written using "scripting" language (think of these as simplified programming languages), such as Netscape's JavaScript, Microsoft's Jscript, VBscript, and others.

Although HTML has been around for 20 years or so, the meteoric rise of the Internet—and especially of the Web—has thrown the language's shortcomings into sharp relief. HTML has evolved into a "new" language called Dynamic HTML (DHTML) with features tailored to recent Web innovations such as JavaScript applets. Web pages that feature a DHTML component will not work on browsers unable to interpret DHTML.

Manipulating HTML and JavaScript directly has one enormous advantage; you have complete control of every aspect of your designs.

However, Web-authoring packages—software that dispenses with HTML and instead provides a WYSIWYG (what-you-see-is-what-you-get) environment in which to create Web page designs—are improving all the time, and now there really is little need to tinker with HTML. Besides, graphic designers work with their eyes, and it's reasonable to assume that they ought to be able to see what it is they are manipulating on-screen. Occasionally, though, there is still no better way to achieve a particular effect than by directly manipulating the raw code.

This book is not aimed at potential programmers. After all, what better way could there be for designers to make the transition to Web design than by using a package similar in style and operation to the DTP software with which they're already completely familiar?

If you want to roll up your sleeves and get your hands dirty doing some coding, there are plenty of excellent programming guides available and several Web sites devoted to teaching you to program in HTML.

CASCADING STYLE SHEETS 1

An enormous problem for designers who gravitate to the Web after creating printed publications is HTML's inability to style and position text with anything like the precision available using DTP software. Master HTML and there's little you can't either do or work around, but still the irritating imprecision remains.

Using HTML, text is individually styled, line by line, using the appropriate tags. For example, a 12–point bold minor heading used as a crosshead in several places on a Web page is styled (at its simplest) using the tag pair <H4> and </H4>, with each occurrence of the crosshead styled using the same tag pair. But what happens if you decide to change the style of your crossheads?

Until recently, blanket changes in style meant selecting and restyling each occurrence individually from within a Web-authoring package, or wading through code with an HTML editor, locating and changing each tag.

Imagine a similar situation using desktop publishing software such as QuarkXPress. Altering a style manually throughout a long document—say, a book or a magazine—would be a thankless task. However, Quark offers the style sheet, a tool taken for granted in the world of desktop publishing. A style sheet enables designers to define a style and apply it to any text in one easy action. Quark also provides the concept of master pages, which define the styles of all subsequent pages based on the master. HTML 4.0 brings the power of both the style sheet and the master page within reach of the Web designer.

Though tailored for use with the peculiarities of Web rather than printed pages, cascading style sheets (or CSS) work in much the same way as ordinary style sheets. You can make block styling changes throughout a Web page or fine-tune a single piece of text at the stroke of a style tag. You can use a style sheet to style the text on a single Web page or create a document of styles and apply it across all the pages of an entire site, thereby making it easy to maintain consistent design.

Cascading style sheets are available in two flavors: internal and external. An internal style sheet is one that can be applied to the text of a single Web document. An external style sheet is applied to any or all of the pages of an entire Web site (and any future Web sites you create).

Both internal and external style sheets break down further. Internal style sheets can be deemed either "embedded" or "inline." The embedded variety appears as a group of styles in the HTML heading of a single Web document, and the styles they specify affect every associated HTML tag throughout the document. Inline styles are inserted into the tag pair of a single style within the document and affect only the text between the tags. In the <H4> example above, an embedded style sheet would affect every occurrence of <H4> text throughout the document, while an inline style would affect just that one instance of <H4>.

External style sheets are available as "linked" or "imported." A linked style sheet is a document containing the styles you want to apply. Using a <LINK> tag, the style sheet document is applied to selected pages. Imported style sheets work in a similar way in that they feature a document of styles linked to Web pages, but they also feature local styles that are applied

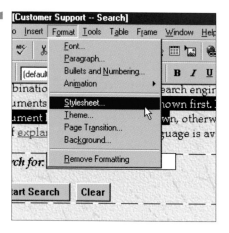

The latest HTML standard provides for style sheets similar to those available in DTP software.

Older browsers are unable to make sense of the embedded CSS code, but placing it between standard comment tags allows it to be ignored by those browsers unable to display it.

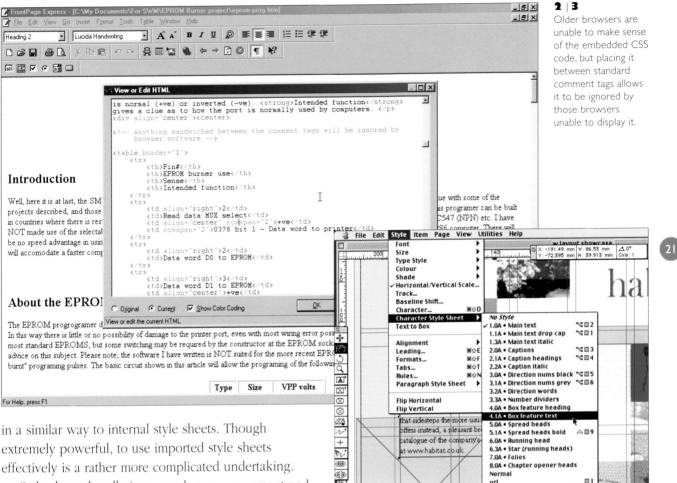

in a similar way to internal style sheets. Though extremely powerful, to use imported style sheets effectively is a rather more complicated undertaking.

Style sheets handle issues such as measurement and color differently from standard HTML. Although CSS supports the usual pixel or percentage measurements of HTML, you can also apply measurements in points, picas, centimeters, ems, and so on. This allows precision measuring that is better than that previously available. Colors, however, are handled poorly in the current CSS1 standard, with a rather limiting 16 colors available from the World Wide Web Consortium's (W3C) standard color palette.

Older browsers, such as Internet Explorer before version 3.x and Netscape Navigator prior to versions 4.x, will not be able to interpret and resolve the scripting language used for CSS. The on-screen results could be surprising to say the least, so it is good

practice to enclose CSS scripting tags within standard HTML comment tags. Although this does not affect the way style sheets work with CSS-enabled browsers, it does enable earlier software to simply sidestep the CSS code. Unfortunately, using comment tags requires you to tinker with source code, but the process is not a difficult one. Simply switch your authoring tool to a source view, locate the CSS <STYLE> tag and type <!— immediately before it. Similarly, at the end of the style sheet script, locate the </STYLE> tag and place —> immediately after it. These HTML comment tags will effectively hide all the CSS script that would otherwise confuse older browsers.

CASCADING STYLE SHEETS 2

The World Wide Web Consortium (W3C) is the organization that defines the standards for HTML. This group defined and implemented HTML 4.0, the version that supports cascading style sheets. CSS itself has also been defined as a standard known as CSS1. This standardization ought to mean that any browser that supports HTML 4.0 will also support CSS.

It will come as no surprise to anyone familiar with the Web that both Microsoft and Netscape have created their own slightly incompatible versions of CSS1, which means there is a chance you will encounter browsers and combinations of styles that won't work as expected.

CSS isn't HTML, but it does use a similar kind of coding system. The CSS code combines with HTML tags and is interpreted by compatible browsers as a homogenized whole. You could use style sheets by entering CSS tags into HTML documents, but only masochists and computer geeks would enjoy the

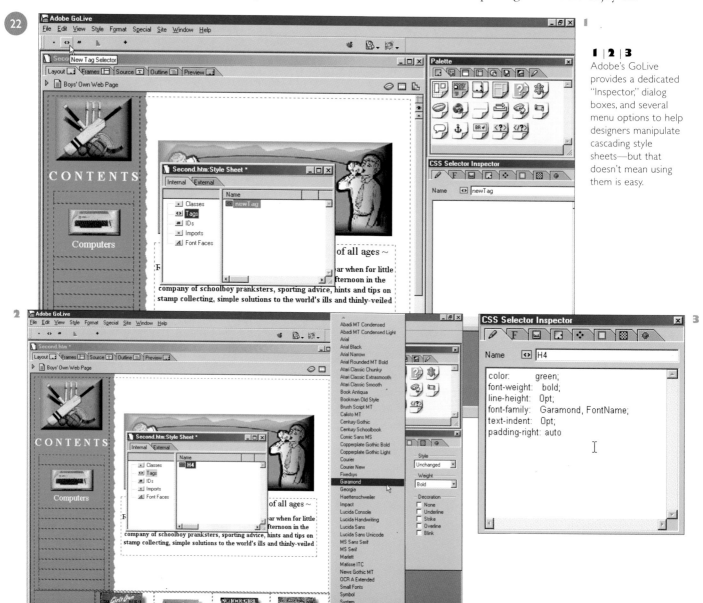

1 | 2 | 3
Adobe's GoLive provides a dedicated "Inspector," dialog boxes, and several menu options to help designers manipulate cascading style sheets—but that doesn't mean using them is easy.

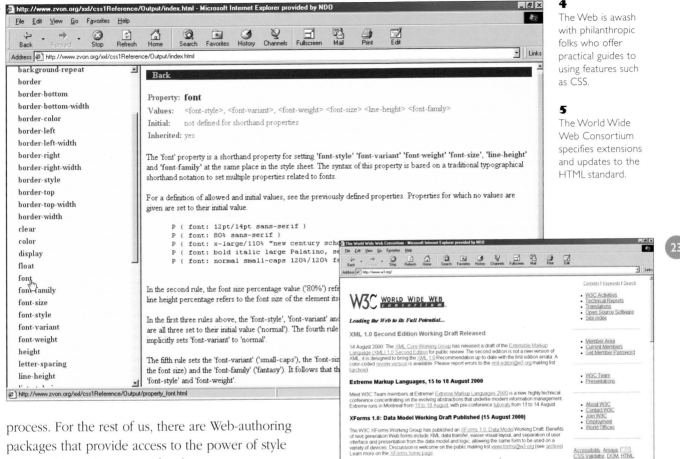

The Web is awash with philanthropic folks who offer practical guides to using features such as CSS.

5
The World Wide Web Consortium specifies extensions and updates to the HTML standard.

process. For the rest of us, there are Web-authoring packages that provide access to the power of style sheets without the agony of coding.

One such product is Adobe's GoLive. Version 4.0 of the program offers lavish access to style sheets via dedicated menu options, dialog boxes, and the GoLive "Inspector." Both internal and external style sheets are available and are created and configured in much the same way as style sheets within a DTP application.

Creating, say, an internal style sheet using GoLive, you would click on the Style Sheet button in the top right corner of an open document. This action summons GoLive's Style Sheet window, which shows available previously created style sheets and clickable tabs for internal and external sheets. The window defaults to "Internal" and displays five fields: Classes, Tags, IDs, Imports, and Font Faces. Three of these—Classes, Tags, and IDs—create style sheets that directly style the

contents of an HTML document. These fields provide quick access to all the style sheets you will create using GoLive's tools.

To create a new style sheet that will style, for example, HTML tags, click the New Tag Selector button on the Style Sheet toolbar. The Tags field in the Style Sheet dialog is highlighted and a new tag style sheet titled "newTag" is displayed. The CSS Inspector is also displayed.

Highlight "newTag" in the Inspector's Name field, give it a suitable name, such as H1 or H4 (or whatever tag it is you want style), and press Enter. Now click each of the tabs in the Inspector in turn and use the options provided by each to determine the style for your new tag style sheet. Preview the results with a browser.

WEB-AUTHORING SOFTWARE 1

Although directly manipulating HTML, JavaScripts, and the like gives comprehensive control over Web design, the process can be a complex and lengthy one for nonprogrammers. HTML's tagging system is verbose, and while the various scripting languages are said to be easier to learn than true computer programming languages, using them effectively requires skills that not everyone has or wishes to learn.

The move by designers to computers and desktop publishing software happened as recently as perhaps ten years ago, and designing exclusively on a computer is

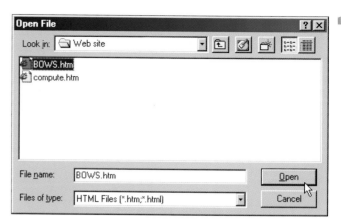

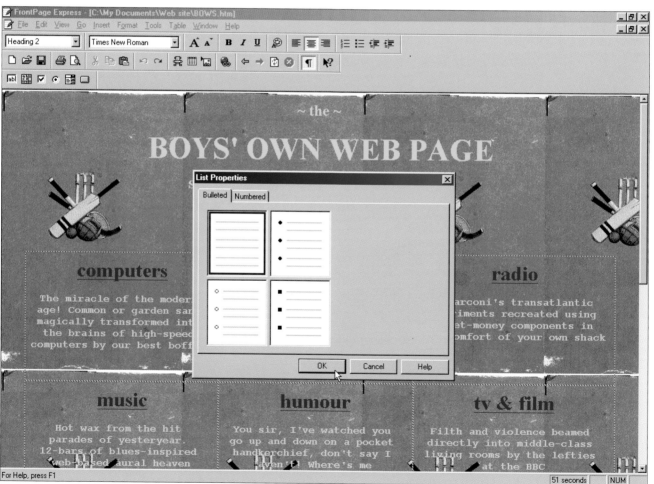

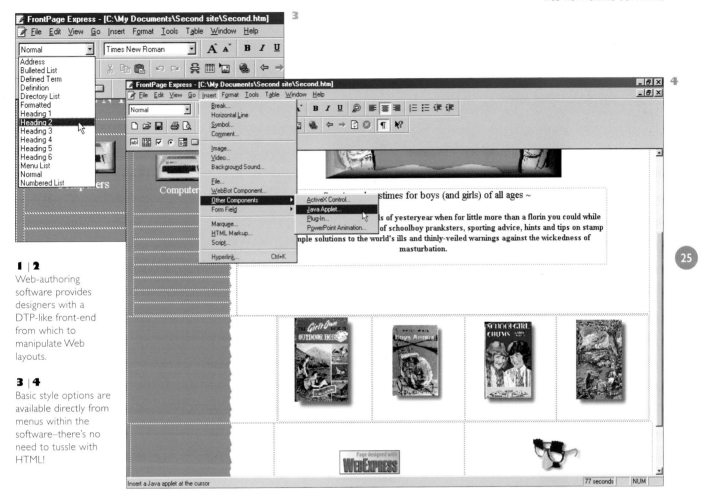

1 | 2
Web-authoring software provides designers with a DTP-like front-end from which to manipulate Web layouts.

3 | 4
Basic style options are available directly from menus within the software–there's no need to tussle with HTML!

considerably more recent than that. Learning to program is not something that the majority of designers should be expected to do or want to do. Fortunately, only those who choose to take up programming have to, because for the rest there is Web-authoring software.

Rather like the popular desktop publishing packages such as QuarkXPress, Web-authoring software offers a WYSIWYG environment in which to create Web pages. Elements such as text and graphics that will appear on the page are imported into a blank "document" just as they are in the DTP software used to design books, magazines, and newspapers.

Unlike DTP software, though, Web-authoring software also provides for the simple creation of Web-specific components such as hyperlinks, rollover buttons, ticker-tape banners, and the like.

Although early offerings were at best simple, recent examples sport much of the typographic control you'd expect from a good-quality DTP program. Additionally, there are usually tools for translating graphics into formats suitable for the Web, automatic organization and tracking of all the files needed for a Web presence into suitable directories, and, typically, even a file transfer protocol (FTP) option from within the program.

Which program you choose depends largely on what you want to achieve, how much money you have to spend, and whether you're locked into the products of a particular supplier, such as Microsoft.

WEB-AUTHORING SOFTWARE 2

The Web-authoring software world is dominated by two major-league players: Microsoft and Adobe. Microsoft's FrontPage is available in several versions, including a "light" version known as FrontPage Express, which comes bundled with the Windows operating system. Though equipped with a limited range of features, FrontPage Express serves as a useful introduction to what is possible using a WYSIWYG Web-authoring package. Better still, it's key-compatible with later and full versions of the software, which means that you have to learn the program's basic command structure only once.

The latest version of Microsoft's FrontPage package is FrontPage 2000. The program is packed with features that exploit the very latest advances in HTML, such as cascading style sheets, and which make the manipulation of everything from frames to forms as easy as selecting from menu options.

The other major player is Adobe, a long-respected name in the world of print publishing and well-known

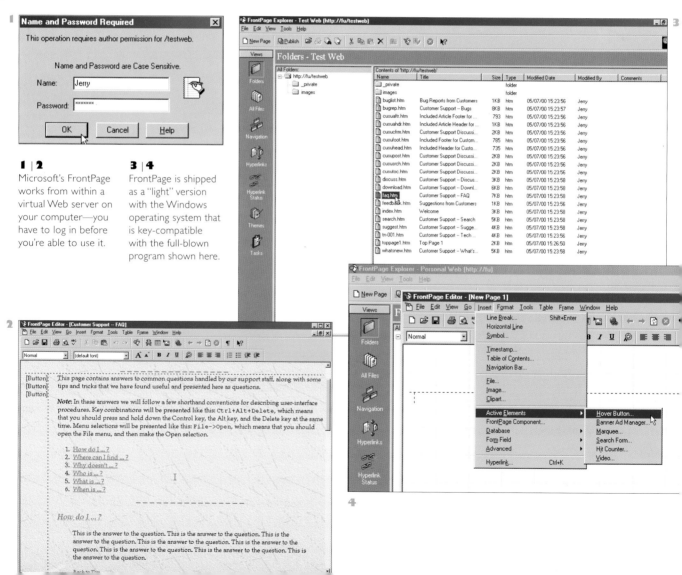

1 | 2
Microsoft's FrontPage works from within a virtual Web server on your computer—you have to log in before you're able to use it.

3 | 4
FrontPage is shipped as a "light" version with the Windows operating system that is key-compatible with the full-blown program shown here.

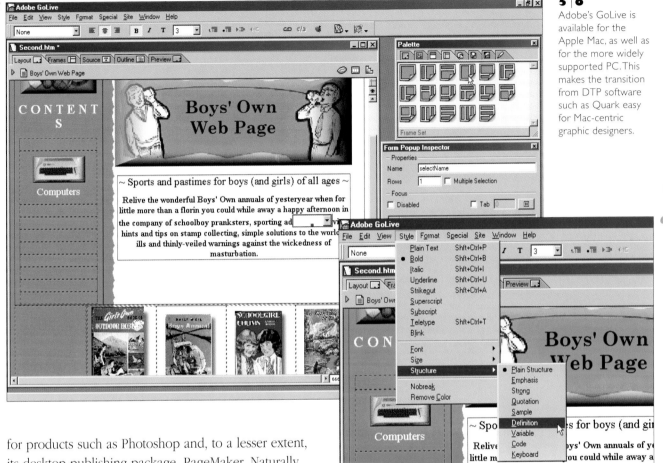

Adobe's GoLive is
available for the
Apple Mac, as well as
for the more widely
supported PC. This
makes the transition
from DTP software
such as Quark easy
for Mac-centric
graphic designers.

for products such as Photoshop and, to a lesser extent,
its desktop publishing package, PageMaker. Naturally,
Adobe has also produced a range of Web-authoring tools,
including PageMill, an easy-to-use package suitable for
home and small business use (recently discontinued but
still popular), and its heavyweight contender for the title
of foremost Web-authoring tool, GoLive.

Available for both Windows and Macintosh
machines, GoLive is comprehensively equipped with
just about everything necessary to create exceptional
Web designs. Intuitive access to cutting-edge features,
such as the all-important cascading style sheets, puts
Adobe GoLive at the top of any buyer's must-have list.
Inevitably, which authoring product you choose

depends on factors other than whether they perform
well design-wise. Cost, brand loyalty, and familiarity all
play their part.

Whichever you decide on, both GoLive and FrontPage
give comprehensive control over Web page makeup.
Both are supported by hundreds of Web sites, provided
and maintained by users of the programs who offer tips
and insights into their chosen software. (The desire to
broadcast an undying brand loyalty is a peculiar feature
of the Web.)

NET OBJECTS

At first glance, a Web page will probably look to you more or less like a printed page, but it's a fleeting similarity. Web pages have all sorts of peculiar and exotic objects embedded in them, many of which it's almost certain that, as a designer, you won't have encountered before. For the most part, the use of these Web-specific objects is entirely logical but, for a time, incorporating them into your designs will be a novel experience.

Most of the Web-specific components on a page are dedicated to the task of enabling visitors to navigate their way to subpages or elsewhere on the Web.

The object you'll encounter most often is a text-based "hyperlink." The hyperlink is the most basic unit of a Web page and is, essentially, the reason why the Web

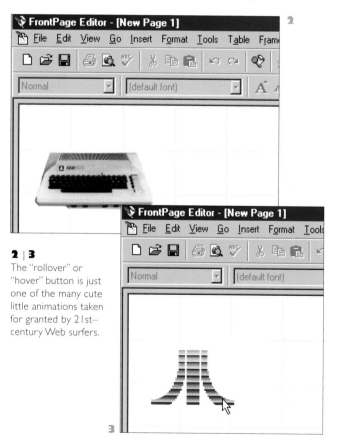

1

w the addition of style sheet information to a Web page easier. Because style sheets, if used properly, help to s urists, to whom document structure is everything.

ion to HTML, and is a standard recommended by the Wc how supported in Internet Explorer 3. *x*, Internet Explor cle Cascading Style Sheets in Internet Explorer 4.0.

dvantages to using CSS over plain HTML:

properties

1
The underlined hyperlink highlighted in blue is the principle reason why the Web exists. It is the single most common Web feature you'll encounter.

2|3
The "rollover" or "hover" button is just one of the many cute little animations taken for granted by 21st–century Web surfers.

exists. The underlying concept of the Web is that it is a linking together of otherwise disparate pieces of information in such a way that—in the words of the Web's creator, Tim Berners-Lee—"a random association between . . . information" is formed.

These associations are constructed using hyperlinks and they are what give the Web its enormous potential and power. You can link a master page at a Web site to subpages on the same site, simplifying its organization, and you can link to other pages anywhere in cyberspace. Also available are "anchor" links, which are used to navigate around a single Web page. A clicked anchor link causes the browser to scroll the page to a specific point elsewhere in the same page. For example, a bulleted list of options is often linked to detailed text elsewhere on the same page.

Until recently, convention dictated that text-based hyperlinks always appeared as blue underlined type. Moving the mouse over the link changes the pointer to a pointing hand symbol; by clicking the underlined text, you are transported to wherever (or whatever) it is linked to. Text hyperlinks activated in this way change color (usually to magenta) to show they've previously been "followed" (though they are still available as links).

Buttons are second in popularity only to text hyperlinks on the Web. Available in endless shapes and styles, buttons act as graphic hyperlinks, and they are found everywhere. You can design your own buttons using a paint package such as Photoshop or Paint Shop

The basic Net objects such as buttons form the basis for some very attractive Web-page effects limited only by your imagination—like the Action Man button flags.

Tinkertoys

Click on the swatch above to see a full repeat of the pattern...
A complete set of swatches is available in the Market.

Pro, or you can buy ready-made examples from many dedicated sites, such as **www.webspice.com**.

Buttons work well as hyperlinked graphics, but they are also used for other purposes. Submit and Reset buttons are used with interactive forms so that visitors can submit information they have entered on a form to the server. A reset button clears the form, enabling the data to be entered again. Radio buttons allow users to select from a range of options, and there are others you'll encounter along the way.

Increasingly, buttons are enlivened further by specifying them as "rollovers." A rollover is a button that changes in some way as the mouse pointer passes over it but without anything having to be clicked. Typical applications include submit buttons that are highlighted when the pointer passes over them, embedded links that change from a light to a darker hue to show that they are "live," images of products that change to display a price, and so on.

Another popular Web component is the ticker-tape streamer (known as a "marquee" in Microsoft parlance). This is a horizontally-scrolling line of text used to catch the attention of visitors and provide information that would be dull if it were static.

DRAWING A BLANK I

The Web, HTML, and the browsers that surf the one and interpret the other combine to produce a fluid medium—guaranteeing that establishing the spatial relationships between Web page components is not an easy task. This fluidity is a factor that a wise designer will use as a base line.

And while each new addition to the HTML standard extends the limits to what you, as a designer, can do on the Web, it also builds in incompatibility with versions that went before it. The relatively recent introduction of cascading style sheets has fine-tuned the precision available to a Web page designer while at the same time excluding those designs from browsers unable to support the HTML 4.0 standard, which provides for CSS. Nowhere are form and function so thoroughly linked than on the Web. As a designer, and especially if you design commercial sites, you must be constantly wary of creating Web designs that effectively exclude all but a small number of visitors who have the latest browsers installed on their machines. Many users continue to rely on old technology with slow processors and limited graphics and sound capabilities. These machines are likely to be running older browsers and using modems that will slow to an unacceptable crawl when they encounter heavily multimedia-oriented Web sites.

It is true that when designing a commercial Web site you can get away with colors, effects, and type styles that no company would ever sanction in its printed publications—the Web is, after all, a young and vibrant medium—but you should control your wilder urges and craft aesthetically pleasing and, above all, usable Web sites.

In the great browser wars, two major players slug it out for supremacy: Microsoft and Netscape. The programmers who became Netscape created the first graphical browser ever—Mosaic—back in the early 1990s. Now, however, Microsoft's browser, Internet Explorer, is used by more people than Netscape's. What

1
Microsoft and Netscape dominate the browser world with their software Internet Explorer and Netscape Navigator. Each has features that are incompatible with the other, which is something you must take into account—especially if you design complicated Web pages that feature lots of effects. Fuse98 **www.fuse98 .com** states on its opening page that its site is oriented toward both browsers.

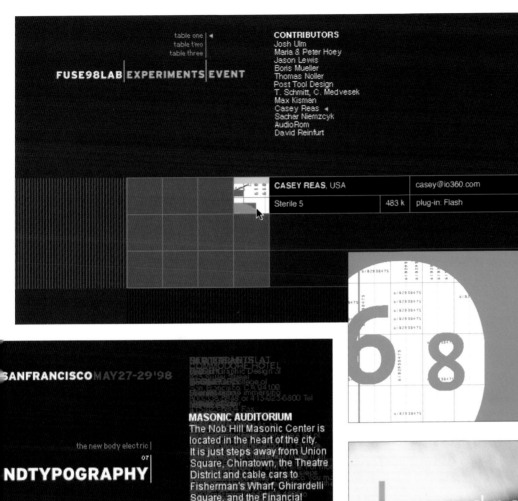

FUSE98LAB|EXPERIMENTS|EVENT

table one ◄
table two
table three

CONTRIBUTORS
Josh Ulm
Maria & Peter Hoey
Jason Lewis
Boris Mueller
Thomas Noller
Post Tool Design
T. Schmitt, C. Medvesek
Max Kisman
Casey Reas ◄
Sachar Niemzcyk
AudioRom
David Reinfurt

CASEY REAS, USA		casey@io360.com
Sterile 5	483 k	plug-in: Flash

2 | 3 | 4 | 5
The www.fuse98
.com site has a
geometric layout
which, though smart
and simple, has
complex building
blocks. It works well
with both browsers,
however, even the
typographic art
featured below.

33

4

5

SANFRANCISCO MAY 27-29 '98

the new body electric |
07
NDTYPOGRAPHY |

MASONIC AUDITORIUM
The Nob Hill Masonic Center is
located in the heart of the city.
It is just steps away from Union
Square, Chinatown, the Theatre
District and cable cars to
Fisherman's Wharf, Ghirardelli
Square, and the Financial
District.

n on the top of Nob Hill, San Francisco.

NOB HILL
This historic neighborhood has
panoramic views of the city, and is
home to Huntington Park, Grace
Cathedral, and the Mark Hopkins
Hotel.

this means for designers is that they should be aware of
the inconsistencies between the two products.

While plain-vanilla Web sites will work fine with
both browsers, those packed with effects may not. It is a
good idea indeed using both browsers to test the
features of your pages for compatibility.

DRAWING A BLANK 2

The first step in designing a book, magazine, or newspaper is to determine factors such as page size, margin widths, the number of columns and their widths, and the measure for images—essentially, the base specifications that combine to produce a grid with which you create a coherent working design.

Designing for the Web is no different. You begin by deciding on a target screen resolution, and it is this resolution that decides the size of your "pages." The next step is to decide whether you want to specify the spatial relationships of the elements on the page on the basis of a pixel count or as a percentage of the overall page space. Each method has advantages and disadvantages.

A pixel count enables you to specify more or less exactly where, for example, a picture will be placed relative to other elements on the page. However, if the page reaches a browser that is set to a screen resolution other than your target—640×480 rather than 800×600, for example—it will be displayed with scroll bars.

Similarly, placing page elements according to a percentage of the available page size will result in their being positioned to suit screen resolution. This can also have unpredictable results.

Currently, there are three popular screen resolutions from which to choose. These are, in pixels: 640×480, 800×600, and 1024×768. Of the three, 800×600 is the current "standard," and designing Web pages to match is a fairly safe bet.

Visitors with browsers set to display at 640×480 will be automatically provided with scroll bars and will have to scroll horizontally and perhaps vertically to see everything contained within your pages. Those with browsers set to a resolution greater than 800×600—say, 1024×768—either will see the pixel-fixed pages with a certain amount of wasted space around the "edges," or, if the measurement parameter is a percentage, the pages will be sized to fit the browser window, with the

A page from AltaVista's Web site, shown here viewed with a fully capable browser.

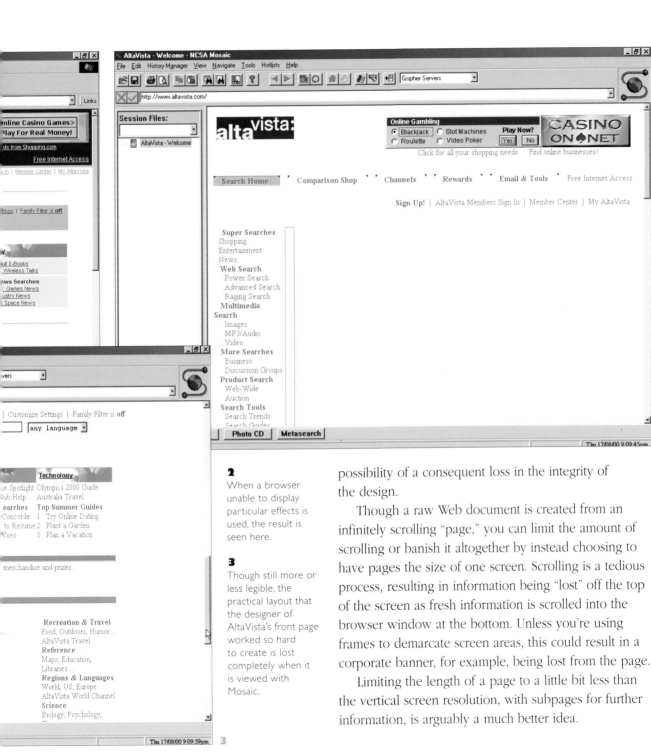

2
When a browser unable to display particular effects is used, the result is seen here.

3
Though still more or less legible, the practical layout that the designer of AltaVista's front page worked so hard to create is lost completely when it is viewed with Mosaic.

possibility of a consequent loss in the integrity of the design.

Though a raw Web document is created from an infinitely scrolling "page," you can limit the amount of scrolling or banish it altogether by instead choosing to have pages the size of one screen. Scrolling is a tedious process, resulting in information being "lost" off the top of the screen as fresh information is scrolled into the browser window at the bottom. Unless you're using frames to demarcate screen areas, this could result in a corporate banner, for example, being lost from the page.

Limiting the length of a page to a little bit less than the vertical screen resolution, with subpages for further information, is arguably a much better idea.

BACKGROUNDS

Arguably, and above all else, a background can make or break a Web page design. Though essential to a strong design, a background can make it extra difficult for visitors to read the text on your Web page—an especially important factor when you consider that reading from a monitor is hard enough on the eyes as it is. Unlike printed publications, monitors flicker at a rate somewhere between 60 and 85 times a second, which, though virtually invisible to the naked eye, induces strain and places a heavy toll on concentration.

Conventional monitors produce their pictures with dots of phosphor at a density far less than even the 300dpi of a standard laser printer. Couple that with the flickering caused by the electron guns striking and illuminating these dots and it is easy to see why eye strain is just an unsuitable background away. Make it difficult for a visitor to read your Web page with an overly complex graphical background and the inevitable result will be visitors who don't visit for long!

Early browsers defaulted to a uniform gray background, which is easy on the eye and offers a high degree of readability. Currently, white is the default background color, and, although most people prefer to

1

1 | 2 | 3
Used carefully, an image makes an excellent background, as in these examples from **www.prophet comm.com** (above) and **www.citroen. com** (right). However, there's nothing quite like a crisp white background **www.damien hirst.co.uk** (left) for getting your message across.

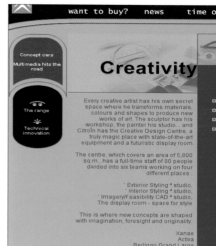

2

3

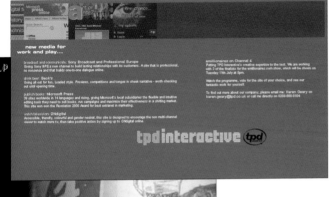

read black text on white backgrounds, the combination is one that induces the most eye strain. Crisp white screens flicker intensely because more (all) of their phosphor dots are being illuminated.

A startling white background can be beautiful and makes the perfect complement for an image map front door page, but avoid white for a screen with lots of text.

At the other extreme of the color wheel, black backgrounds give immense depth to a Web page, providing an almost tangible feeling of space. But black should not be used with pages containing lots of text—at least, not without serious consideration. For all hues between black and white, rely on your designer's sense of what's right and let your watchword be legibility.

As well as using uniform colors as backgrounds, it is entirely possible to use a picture or a pattern created with image-editing software. Browsers tile an image that is smaller than one screen, which can produce many aesthetically pleasing effects.

4

www.tpd.co.uk uses rich colors with care and ensures that text remains legible.

5

By using image-editing software such as Paint Shop Pro, you can knock back an image or apply an effect, such as embossing or buttonizing, to create a striking background that is attractive but doesn't swamp the message. www.kitsch.co.uk is one example of a site that creates this effect.

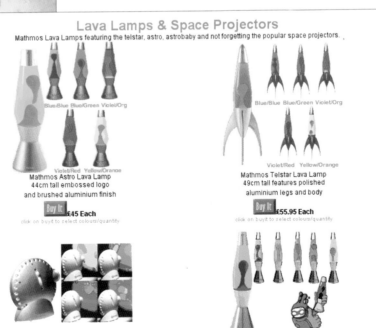

BUILDING BLOCKS

Essentially, HTML is a tagging method for styling text, and although it is true that the system has evolved into a comprehensive "programming language" for Web pages, specifying a precise layout remains a somewhat hit–and–miss affair. Rely on a visitor's browser to position your delicately crafted design and you can more or less kiss it goodbye. Those who like to tinker with HTML code can use <PRE> tags to specify "precise" relationships between columns; but given that tabbing to space isn't recommended, entering the text as columns is a tedious process, and results still can't be guaranteed. That's why using tables as a fundamental unit of design is a good idea.

An HTML table is a grid consisting of rows and columns of cells into which you place and precisely position text, a picture, a QuickTime movie clip, form components, or any other Web page element. It is even possible to nest tables (that is, place a table within a table) for ever more precise positioning of Web components. The table is a way to give the appearance of multicolumn

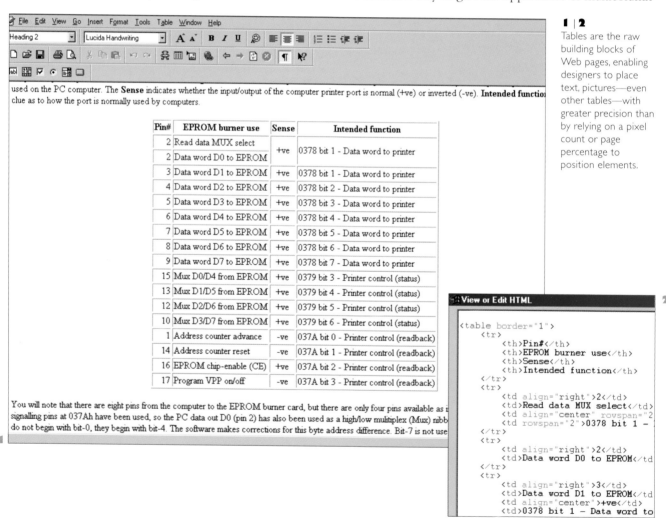

1 | 2

Tables are the raw building blocks of Web pages, enabling designers to place text, pictures—even other tables—with greater precision than by relying on a pixel count or page percentage to position elements.

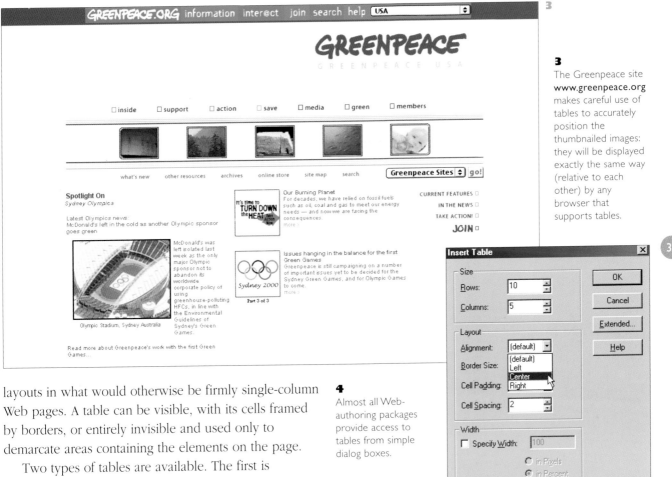

3
The Greenpeace site **www.greenpeace.org** makes careful use of tables to accurately position the thumbnailed images: they will be displayed exactly the same way (relative to each other) by any browser that supports tables.

39

layouts in what would otherwise be firmly single-column Web pages. A table can be visible, with its cells framed by borders, or entirely invisible and used only to demarcate areas containing the elements on the page.

Two types of tables are available. The first is specified with a pixel count that fixes its size irrespective of the browser or screen resolution it is viewed with. This is fine if you want to maintain precise relationships between components in your designs, but it might compel a visitor to scroll around your page to see all the information in the table.

Tables can also be specified as a percentage of the available screen space. The visitor's browser resizes the table to fit the screen resolution. The potential need to scroll is removed, but you can't be sure what the result will look like.

Be aware that with a slow Internet connection, a large table may cause an unacceptable pause while it is resolved on a visitor's machine, with the result that for several minutes only the background is displayed while

4
Almost all Web-authoring packages provide access to tables from simple dialog boxes.

the table is downloaded. Those with short attention spans may well have moved on in the meantime.

GoLive takes the table-as-a-positioning-tool concept a stage further. The program provides what it calls a "layout grid," which is positioned and sized on a Web document. You can drag and drop Web page elements, such as text, images, form elements, buttons, and the like, anywhere on the grid. Viewing the results with a browser shows only a multicolumn Web page layout, but behind the scenes GoLive has translated the relative positions of the elements on the layout grid into precise HTML tables, automating what would otherwise be a manual—and extremely tedious—task.

BASIC TEXT ISSUES 1

Though the Web is almost invariably touted as a multimedia experience, with colorful images, exciting animations, live video, streaming sound, and all the other effects that spring to mind, the fact remains that its most important part—certainly the part that most Web masters are striving to make you aware of when you visit their sites—is the text. Surf the Web for even a few minutes, and you will be regaled with everything from extensive personal histories to novels, Ph.D. theses, product advertising, and even on-line absolution. Few are the sites without words of some description. A picture might well be worth a thousand words, but in cyberspace, a detailed image requires an awfully long time to download—and in that time far more than a thousand words can be delivered.

The Web was created to make the manipulation of

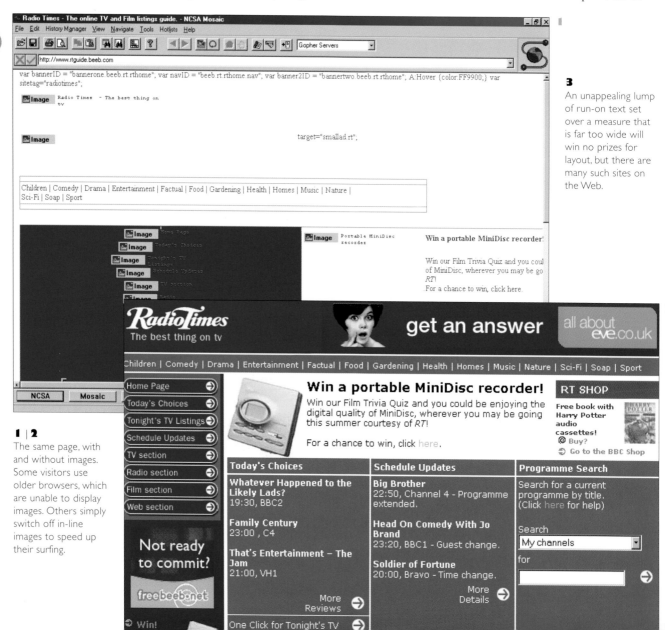

3

An unappealing lump of run-on text set over a measure that is far too wide will win no prizes for layout, but there are many such sites on the Web.

1 | 2

The same page, with and without images. Some visitors use older browsers, which are unable to display images. Others simply switch off in-line images to speed up their surfing.

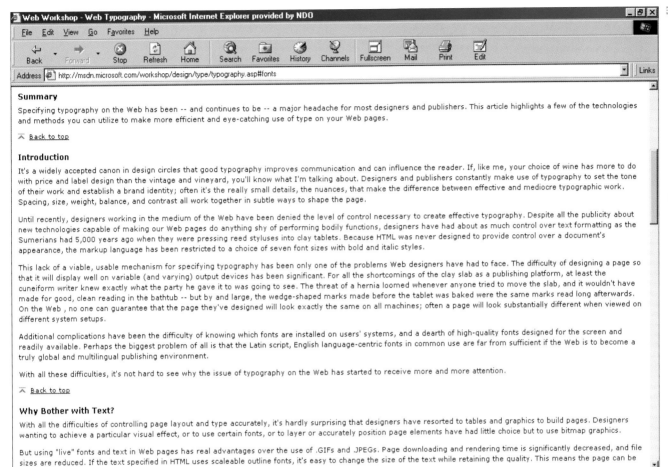

Summary

Specifying typography on the Web has been -- and continues to be -- a major headache for most designers and publishers. This article highlights a few of the technologies and methods you can utilize to make more efficient and eye-catching use of type on your Web pages.

⌃ Back to top

Introduction

It's a widely accepted canon in design circles that good typography improves communication and can influence the reader. If, like me, your choice of wine has more to do with price and label design than the vintage and vineyard, you'll know what I'm talking about. Designers and publishers constantly make use of typography to set the tone of their work and establish a brand identity; often it's the really small details, the nuances, that make the difference between effective and mediocre typographic work. Spacing, size, weight, balance, and contrast all work together in subtle ways to shape the page.

Until recently, designers working in the medium of the Web have been denied the level of control necessary to create effective typography. Despite all the publicity about new technologies capable of making our Web pages do anything shy of performing bodily functions, designers have had about as much control over text formatting as the Sumerians had 5,000 years ago when they were pressing reed styluses into clay tablets. Because HTML was never designed to provide control over a document's appearance, the markup language has been restricted to a choice of seven font sizes with bold and italic styles.

This lack of a viable, usable mechanism for specifying typography has been only one of the problems Web designers have had to face. The difficulty of designing a page so that it will display well on variable (and varying) output devices has been significant. For all the shortcomings of the clay slab as a publishing platform, at least the cuneiform writer knew exactly what the party he gave it to was going to see. The threat of a hernia loomed whenever anyone tried to move the slab, and it wouldn't have made for good, clean reading in the bathtub -- but by and large, the wedge-shaped marks made before the tablet was baked were the same marks read long afterwards. On the Web , no one can guarantee that the page they've designed will look exactly the same on all machines; often a page will look substantially different when viewed on different system setups.

Additional complications have been the difficulty of knowing which fonts are installed on users' systems, and a dearth of high-quality fonts designed for the screen and readily available. Perhaps the biggest problem of all is that the Latin script, English language-centric fonts in common use are far from sufficient if the Web is to become a truly global and multilingual publishing environment.

With all these difficulties, it's not hard to see why the issue of typography on the Web has started to receive more and more attention.

⌃ Back to top

Why Bother with Text?

With all the difficulties of controlling page layout and type accurately, it's hardly surprising that designers have resorted to tables and graphics to build pages. Designers wanting to achieve a particular visual effect, or to use certain fonts, or to layer or accurately position page elements have had little choice but to use bitmap graphics.

But using "live" fonts and text in Web pages has real advantages over the use of .GIFs and .JPEGs. Page downloading and rendering time is significantly decreased, and file sizes are reduced. If the text specified in HTML uses scaleable outline fonts, it's easy to change the size of the text while retaining the quality. This means the page can be printed out without the text becoming jagged.

text using arbitrary and random links a reality, and it is a creation which has given everyone, from bedroom-bound computer geeks to global corporations, the freedom to publish their wares quickly, easily, and cheaply, with the potential for a truly global audience.

The very earliest browsers had little or no support for static images and none at all for the kind of multimedia extravaganza we take for granted today. Many people—principally those with older machines—continue to use text-only browsers, such as the venerable Lynx, completely bypassing pictures of any kind. An obvious consequence is that when a text-only browser encounters a site that relies on pictures to convey its message, the result is a confusing and sometimes completely garbled site that makes very little sense.

Some visitors choose to surf the Web with their automatic browser image-loading switched off. This speeds their journeys over the digital superhighway, but can result in problems similar to those experienced by users of text-only browsers. The solution is to ensure that the essential points of your pages are conveyed as text as well as (or instead of) images.

BASIC TEXT ISSUES 2

Images are an enormously important part of the Web designer's arsenal, but words are worth a thousand of them—and will be for the foreseeable future!

Though Web page text is economical in comparison to images, it nevertheless requires a certain amount of download time to reach a visitor's computer. Pages with masses of text—those featuring lengthy reports for example—will take a noticeable time to be resolved in the browser's window. And what is more, lots of tedious scrolling is required to read it all.

Two possible solutions present themselves: to break up the text into screen-sized chunks and present each as a subpage from a home page, with a menu of links or maybe a button bar, or to instead use anchors.

A home page with subpages is an especially neat solution. You can theme the pages so that they are consistent, and elect to have the subpages open in new browser windows so that the home page remains on screen. And if there's an eye-catching banner or a headline on the home page, so much the better!

An anchor is a special type of hyperlink that transports the browser to another part of the same Web page rather than to a subpage or another site elsewhere on the Web. A disadvantage is that all the text must be downloaded to the visitor's browser before the anchor will work, but most visitors would consider that a small price to pay for the convenience of being able to scroll immediately to a point in the text that interests them.

Anchors can be used to mark crossheads or simply to counterpoint what is going on in the body copy.

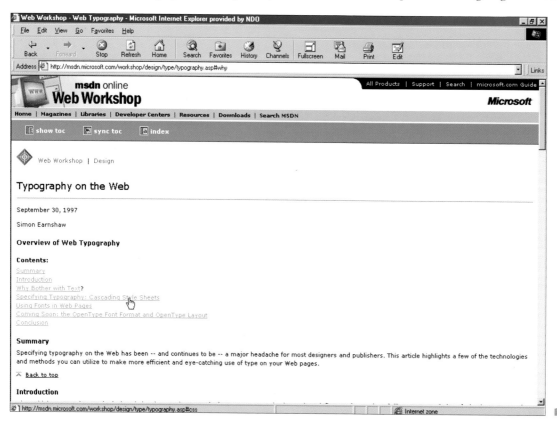

1
Anchors are a special type of hyperlink that points to another position on the same Web page.

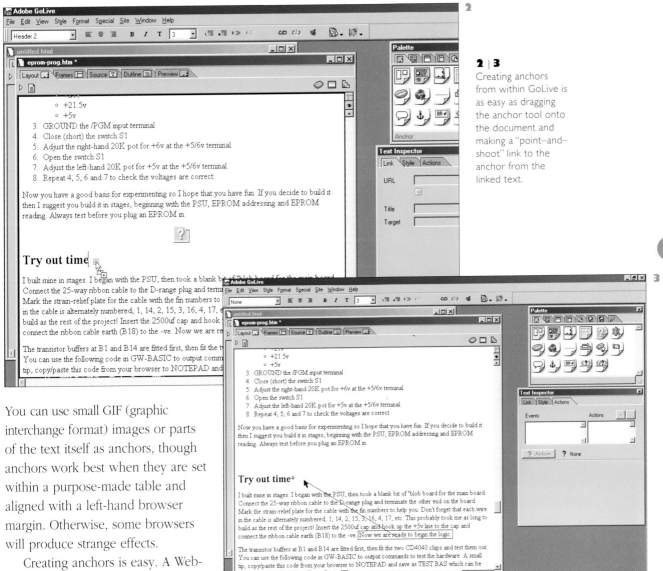

2 | 3
Creating anchors from within GoLive is as easy as dragging the anchor tool onto the document and making a "point–and–shoot" link to the anchor from the linked text.

You can use small GIF (graphic interchange format) images or parts of the text itself as anchors, though anchors work best when they are set within a purpose-made table and aligned with a left-hand browser margin. Otherwise, some browsers will produce strange effects.

Creating anchors is easy. A Web-authoring tool such as GoLive offers two methods: drag the anchor tool to your proposed link point, and then use the Inspector to specify the origin of the link; or simply use GoLive's "point–and–shoot" technique to make the link directly.

Though the technology is improving all the time, it is fair to say that a computer screen is not an ideal medium from which to read text. You should ensure that text—especially anything more than a couple of hundred words—is made as legible as possible by making sensible paragraph breaks and restricting the measure to something less than half the available screen width.

Under no circumstances (at least, no ordinary circumstances!) should your text measure be wider than the screen measure for which you are designing. The result of that is a horizontal scroll bar and the need to move the text from left to right, line by line, which is neither intuitive nor pleasant.

MORE TEXT

The Web is accessed by visitors using many different computers—all without the designer having any idea what these will be. Though it is reasonable to assume that the vast majority are using PC-compatible machines running a flavor of Microsoft Windows, others use antique PCs with text-only browsers, Apple Macs, Atari STs, Commodore Amigas, and Unix boxes of many types. All of them, ostensibly, are incompatible with each other, but they are brought together by the platform-independent glue which is the Internet.

What all this means for the Web designer is that you should strive to make your sites as generic as possible so as not to limit their appeal to potential visitors. Over the past few years there has been some effort to create a vectoring method to ensure the compatibility of typefaces across a number of platforms. The result is

partially successful, but some fonts will still stop a computer in its silicon tracks, and there's no guarantee that a given font will work on both PCs and Macs.

Web page text is rendered (displayed) by a browser with the fonts it has at its disposal, sometimes with little regard for the fonts chosen by the designer. A Web page that includes, for example, Arial and Century Schoolbook on a PC will be rendered perfectly on another PC (if the machine has the fonts installed or if they were downloaded with the page). When visited by someone with an Atari ST, however, the text is rendered with whatever platform-specific font (usually a copy of the well-known typefaces) is available to the machine's browser and operating system. Bold and italic text will be either resolved correctly or simply ignored, depending on whether the browser has those styles at its disposal.

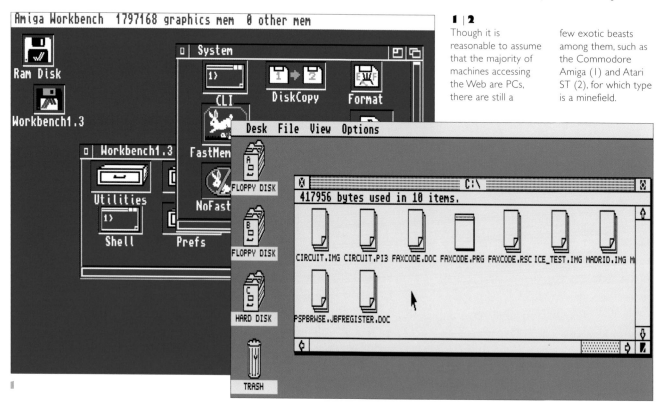

1 | 2
Though it is reasonable to assume that the majority of machines accessing the Web are PCs, there are still a few exotic beasts among them, such as the Commodore Amiga (1) and Atari ST (2), for which type is a minefield.

Trebuchet MS, **Trebuchet MS Bold**, *Trebuchet MS Italic*, ***Bold Italic***

Trebuchet MS, designed by Vincent Connare in 1996, is a humanist sans serif designed for easy screen readability. Trebuchet takes its inspiration from the sans serifs of the 1930s which had large x heights and round features intended to promote readability on signs.

- *download* - Trebuchet MS for Windows 95, 98 and Windows NT
  locations - current server | Redmond | Tokyo | London
  file details - trebuc32.exe - 222KB self installing file
  font details - version 1.15 - Win ANSI + Turkish

- *download* - Trebuchet MS for Windows 3.1 and 3.11
  locations - current server | Redmond | Tokyo | London | ftp
  file details - trebuc.exe - 174KB self extracting archive
  font details - version 1.00

Microsoft *Weft*

Version 5.3.0

3
Microsoft offers a selection of good-quality typefaces, specifically intended for Web use, available for free download from its site. Among them is Trebuchet.
4
The company is also working on a strategy for embedding fonts known as WEFT

47

And while it is true that the ratio of PC to ST visitors is so biased in favor of the PC that the problem is hardly worth considering, it nevertheless illustrates the near-impossibility of guaranteeing the way text on a Web page will be resolved.

A safe bet is to restrict the body copy in your designs to Times and Helvetica and convert anything out of the ordinary—a headline in Garamond with a drop shadow—to a GIF image. This will go some way to ensuring that your pages will be rendered just as they left your Web-authoring tool.

Safe, but potentially dull. Another solution is toward download the fonts along with the associated Web page; but breaching copyright becomes a real issue, though the technique is fine for use with copyright-free fonts.

The type manufacturer Bitstream has a "Truedoc" system, which uses a browser plug-in alongside what it calls "portable font resources" (PFR). These enable an image of the fonts to be transmitted along with a Web page and displayed accurately at the destination.

However, the font can't be used in any other application on the visitor's machine. This neatly avoids the copyright issue while solving the problem of resolving fonts.

Typically, Microsoft has created its own version of this idea, which is called WEFT (Web Embedding Font Tool). This offers four levels of licensing, which range from fonts that can be freely installed on the visitor's computer to fonts that are restricted to display within the browser. WEFT has the advantage of not requiring a plug-in before it can be used.

Microsoft also makes a number of fonts specially for Web use available for free download from its site. These include the popular Verdana, Georgia, Webdings, and Arial Black, and go some way toward making attractive typefaces that are relatively compatible across machines accessing the Web.

There are also lots and lots (and lots!) of copyright-free fonts that you can acquire from magazine-mounted CDs and from the Web itself. These can be downloaded to visitors' machines without problems.

PLACING TEXT

Strangely for designers familiar with precision DTP tools such as QuarkXPress, standard HTML does not specify font size as an absolute measurement in points. Instead, size is expressed in one of seven magnitudes (body, heading 1, heading 2, and so on), which are relative to one another and correspond vaguely to "standard" font sizes (10, 12, 14, 18 pt, and so on). Even the sophisticated Web-authoring tools that provide a WYSIWYG front-end for designing pages must conform to the type rules of HTML. And the problem of accurately specifying type doesn't end there: expressing a font in one of the HTML sizes does not guarantee the size at which it is displayed when it is received by a visitor's browser; most browsers allow visitors to switch the text in the browser window into a "large," "medium," or "small" view.

Using cascading style sheets, it is possible to specify Web page text in absolute terms—font, size, and color—but CSS works with only HTML 4.*x*-enabled browsers; even then, the font is only displayed if it is installed on the visitor's computer. In a bid to work around the worst excesses of Web font use and abuse, Adobe's GoLive authoring tool offers "font sets." Similar fonts are grouped together, applied to a Web document and can be made to substitute for one another if the first-choice font does not exist on the visitor's computer.

Without the use of cascading style sheets, HTML offers limited and generally imprecise text formatting when compared with DTP software for printed publishing. The standard options enable you to create headlines in six sizes, apply physical and logical styles to text, indent it, and create a list. Physical styles are those that you would recognize from the real world, such as italic and bold. They are displayed in much the same way by all browsers. Logical styles are browser-specific and include such esoteric offerings as "emphasis" and "strong." How these are displayed depends very much

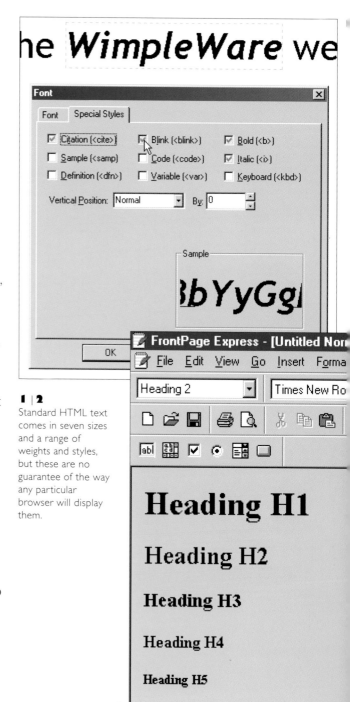

1 | 2
Standard HTML text comes in seven sizes and a range of weights and styles, but these are no guarantee of the way any particular browser will display them.

2

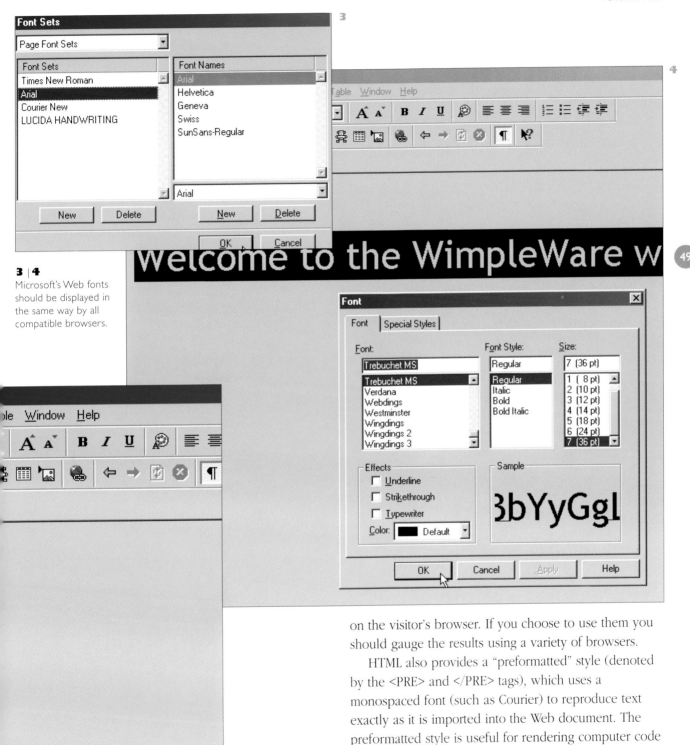

3 | 4
Microsoft's Web fonts
should be displayed in
the same way by all
compatible browsers.

on the visitor's browser. If you choose to use them you
should gauge the results using a variety of browsers.

HTML also provides a "preformatted" style (denoted
by the <PRE> and </PRE> tags), which uses a
monospaced font (such as Courier) to reproduce text
exactly as it is imported into the Web document. The
preformatted style is useful for rendering computer code
and other text where exact reproduction is required.

TEXT AS IMAGES

There is no doubt that the latest HTML 4.0 standard and its support for cascading style sheets gives previously unheard-of precision when styling and positioning text. But when it reaches a visitor's browser the result can still be a hit-and-miss affair.

To ensure that visitors have the required typefaces, you can download fonts to their computers; but then the difficult question of copyright comes into play: fonts belong to someone—usually a corporate "someone," with the necessary weight to litigate successfully. Even if the fonts are copyright-free and you successfully download them to a visitor's machine, there is still no guarantee that a browser will display them in the way you intended.

The solution is to create the text effect you want—a headline, say—and then to convert it to an image file. The image is downloaded and displayed just as it was when it left the server, with all doubt removed about how it will reproduce. The files of images made from text are usually small, so there is little overhead for visitors downloading text images. The image manipulation software you use to create an image from text—Photoshop, Paint Shop Pro, and so on—works with all the fonts you have installed on your computer, and can happily produce virtually any text effect you choose to use. It has to be said, though, that the process is more like freehand drawing than typesetting.

An alternative is to create your text with a traditional DTP package such as QuarkXPress, save the result as an EPS file, and use a paint package or one of the dedicated image conversion utilities (such as GraphicConverter for the Mac) to convert the file to a GIF. Although this method is clunky, it works, and Quark is infinitely better-suited to typesetting than the average paint package—even the good examples, such as the two mentioned above.

Converting text to images works best as a way to capture a single headline or some other relatively small text effect. If you want to reproduce entire pages of text, consider using a dedicated product such as Adobe's Acrobat software. This translates typeset files into what are known as portable document format (PDF) files, which can be displayed and manipulated.

1
Use an image editing program, such as Paint Shop Pro, to translate text to images.

2
Otherwise style your text with a DTP program, such as QuarkXPress, and save it as an EPS file, converting it to a GIF afterwards with a suitable utility.

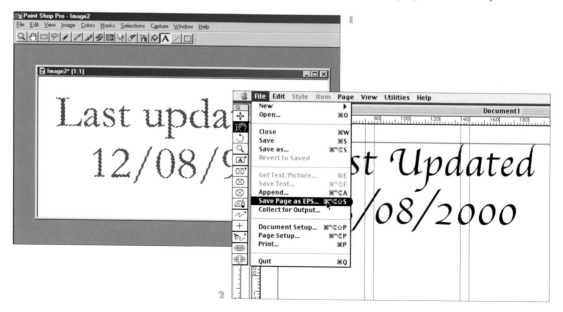

3
Beautifully styled text is all very well, but it may not be rendered as you intended when it reaches a visitor's browser. The solution is to make an image of the text and download the image to visitors' browsers. That way, the "type" will be displayed correctly.

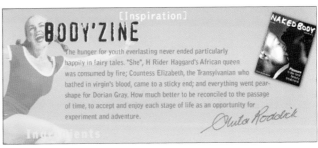

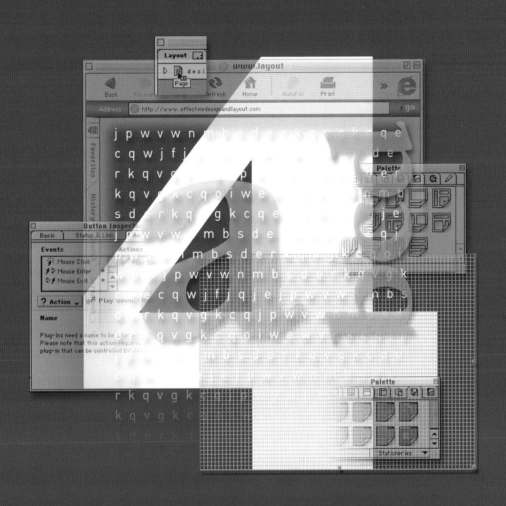

WEB GRAPHICS

Initially, what became the Web we know today was essentially a text-only medium, and early versions of HTML made little provision for manipulating graphics. Subsequent versions have made it increasingly easy to incorporate images into Web pages—and rightly so, for the Web is nothing if not an intensely visual medium.

Graphics transcend the language barrier, enabling visitors from around the world to experience, enjoy, and make productive use of Web sites that might otherwise be beyond their understanding.

There is, however, a downside: images can take a long time to travel across the Web, and a visitor might move on before a page has finished loading. Then—no matter how pretty your site is or how many language barriers you have broken—you've lost your audience.

Among the many digital image file types, several have either been designed especially for the Internet or become adopted by it as "standards." Principal among these are the GIF and the JPEG formats. GIF is an acronym that stands for Graphics Interchange Format. First used on CompuServe, the GIF is a 256-color format ideally suited to representing icons, bullets, cartoons— essentially anything that doesn't require realistic color display, such as a digitized photograph.

The GIF format uses compression techniques based on color redundancy, which help keep the resulting file small; small files translate to minimum download time. There are in fact two GIF standards, known as GIF-87a and GIF-89a. The 89a variety is an extension of the basic GIF format, offering interlacing and transparency, both of which are attractive attributes for Web designers.

A downloaded image is displayed only after all the digital information that makes up the picture has been received by the browser. Large images can take several minutes to download—an unacceptable wait for many users, who will simply click a link to another page.

To obviate the problem, GIF-89a images can be

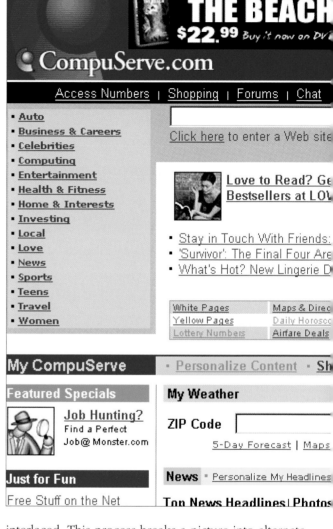

interlaced. This process breaks a picture into alternate "bands" one pixel high. The browser first receives one complete set (bands 2, 4, 6, 8, and so on) and then the other set. Receiving both sets of bands takes roughly the same time as receiving the whole image in the first place, but the process enables a browser to display the picture as a fuzzy, though recognizable, image before it is fully received—no boring wait while the image downloads.

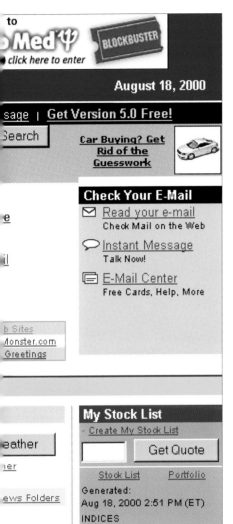

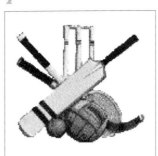

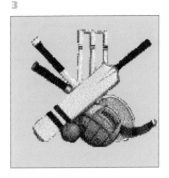

2 | 3
Transparency rids an
image of unwanted
background color,
leaving only the parts
of the image you
want to be displayed.

1
Pages cluttered with
images, buttons, and
banners can take so
long to download to
a browser that the
visitor will move on.

Given its heritage, it is hardly surprising that the JPEG format was devised as a way to store photographic images. Consequently, a JPEG almost invariably results in a better-quality image than the same image rendered as a GIF. JPEGs have a greater color depth (typically 16.7 million colors, compared with a GIF's paltry 256), yet the format results in small files due to its sophisticated compression technique.

Though standard JPEGs can't be interlaced like GIFs, a recent advance in the format, known as the "progressive JPEG," produces a similar effect. An approximation of the JPEG appears in the visitor's browser window, and its clarity is progressively increased until the original image is fully displayed.

Choose JPEGs when you want to display photo-real images, but keep in mind that large images may require extreme download times even though JPEGs feature better compression. JPEGs are inferior to GIFs for rendering text and images that feature blocked colors or sharp lines.

A recent innovation in Web image formats is the PNG (or Portable Network Graphics) format. Because it uses a highly sophisticated compression technique, the PNG format is said to result in file sizes that are typically 30 percent smaller than those for comparable GIFs. As a result, the PNG is being touted as the Web image format of the future. However, older browsers are unable to display PNGs.

Transparency allows the designer to blend GIFs into the background. A small cartoon of, say, a computer, that is used as an icon will be displayed as a computer, not as a cartoon computer inside an oblong background of its own (see the illustrations elsewhere on this page).

The second most popular Web image file format is that devised by the Joint Photographic Experts Group and which carries the group's name: JPEG. (Images rendered as JPEGs are recognized by their .jpg filename.)

PLACING IMAGES 1

No Web page would be complete without at least one attractive image (though how you define "attractive" is open to debate!). Hazy copyright rules make it easy for anyone to acquire pictures, icons, logos, and the like from existing Web sites. In fact, many Web masters actively encourage you to copy their stuff. However, it is simple courtesy (and a wise move if you want to avoid the potential for litigation) to confirm via e-mail that "borrowing" an image is permissible before you make off with it. Also, cheap clip-art CDs (and Web sites) feature vast quantities of copyright-free images that you can use.

Another method of acquiring images is to use a flat-bed scanner. Almost all designers familiar with DTP will have experience using a scanner, and probably either own one or have access to a suitable device. Those

without one, take heart: the flat-bed scanner is currently one of the cheapest peripherals you can buy.

Armed with a scanner and an image, you will be faced with a choice between quality and small file size—you can't have both at once. Scan your image at 100 percent and at the smallest dpi rating you can manage without losing too much of the original resolution of the image—if it looks too pixelated, crank up the scanner's dpi rate. Around 72 dpi is a good starting point.

With a scanned image on-screen you can begin the editing process: crop it, optimize brightness and contrast, and reduce the size of the resulting file as far as possible. File size is dictated by the actual measurements of the image, its file format (GIF or JPEG), color depth, and resolution. Each must be balanced to create the most attractive image, but with the smallest possible file size.

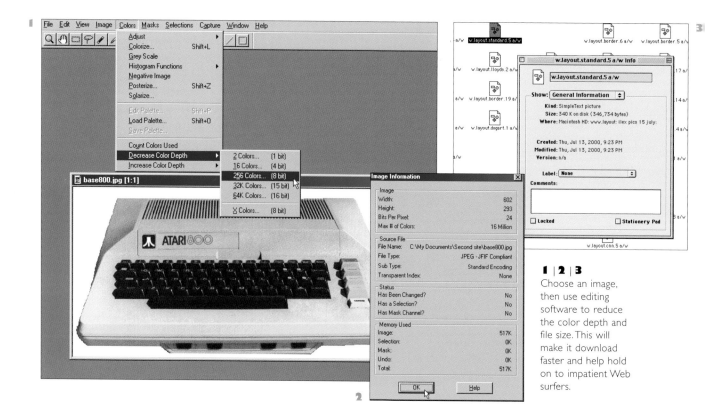

1 | 2 | 3
Choose an image, then use editing software to reduce the color depth and file size. This will make it download faster and help hold on to impatient Web surfers.

5 | 6
Pictures can give
a good sense of
what's to come,
as with retroactive's
front page
**www.modernauction.
com**. Kodak's
frontpage **www.
kodak.com** brings
vacation memories
alive.

4
Pictures make a
powerful statement
and help to break
down language
barriers. The baby
hasn't much to do

with a phone directory
**www.yellowpages.co.
uk**, but the image is
eye-catching and
makes a good visual
joke.

Your aim is to reduce every graphic to a file no
bigger than 30K. With two or three graphics on a page
and file sizes in excess of about 50K, you will suffer
download times that will alienate your site visitors.

If your image is a scanned photograph, save it as a
JPEG and reduce its color depth to 16-bit and 64K. If
you find that color saturation is compromised, increase
the color depth to 16.7 million colors at a depth of
24-bit. Crop out all unwanted details and use your
editing software (Paint Shop Pro, Adobe Photoshop, etc.)
to resize the image to suit your page design. Save the
image. Back on the computer desktop, right-click (if
using a PC) the newly saved image file, select Properties,
and read off the file size. Alternatively, on the Mac
desktop, click the image and press Command-I.

① No bigger
30 K

③ Size the image.
160 × 60 @ 75dpi

② ✓ Save as Gif or PNG

substitute another image if the download time of the
original really is unacceptable.

Graphics other than scanned photographs should be
saved as GIFs or possibly PNGs. Crop unwanted detail
as explained, resize the image to suit your design, and
reduce the color depth as far possible without
compromising the final image. As before, determine the
file size from the desktop.

PLACING IMAGES 2

Access time is a constant issue for wary Web designers—especially when working with images. Even a one-minute wait while a graphic wends its way across the Web will result in visitors clicking off your page before it has downloaded. There are several strategies you can use with images to obviate this problem, one of which is known as transparency.

When a browser displays a Web page, it gradually acquires each packet of data necessary to reconstitute the Web page as it is stored at the server. Text appears almost instantly, but images take longer. Until all the data for an images have been received, it won't be displayed in the browser window—an often unacceptable situation. Small images are not a problem, but larger examples—perhaps the central image on your page—seem to take forever at peak Net access times.

Fortunately, it is possible to specify a GIF image as

"interlaced" and to have a progressively more detailed version of it appear each time a packet of data is received by the browser. This results in a picture—albeit a low-resolution, hazy rendition—appearing almost instantly, inhibiting the desire of an impatient Web surfer to click ahead and thereby miss your message.

Interlaced GIFs are broken up into alternate strips of picture data, one pixel deep. One group of strips—1, 3, 5, 7 or 2, 4, 6, 8, etc.—is sent first, followed by the second set. This enables the browser to render a low-resolution but recognizable image very quickly.

Though standard JPEGs can't be interlaced, you can save them as "progressive JPEGs," and the resulting files are received by a browser in much the same way as interlaced GIFs. Packets of data build the JPEG into ever-clearer renditions of the image until all the data have been received and the image is displayed fully defined.

You can use Web-authoring software, such as Microsoft's FrontPage, to automatically create thumbnails, providing better organization of a site.

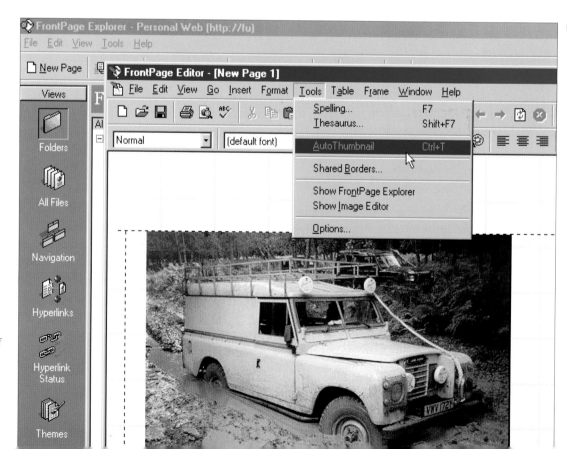

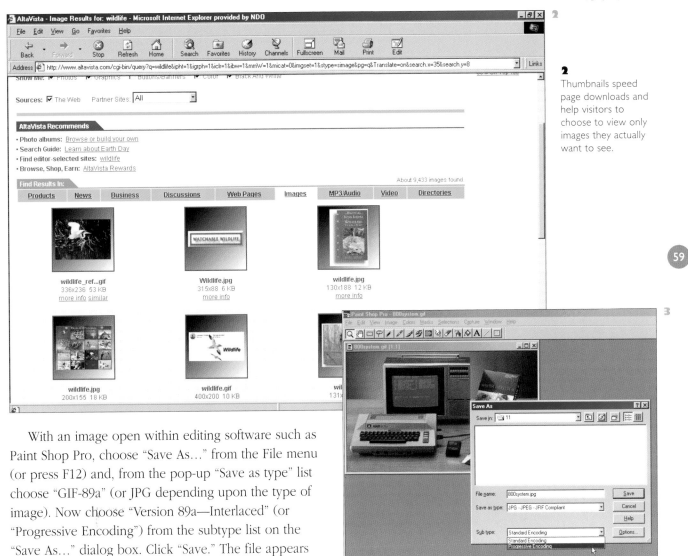

2
Thumbnails speed page downloads and help visitors to choose to view only images they actually want to see.

59

With an image open within editing software such as Paint Shop Pro, choose "Save As…" from the File menu (or press F12) and, from the pop-up "Save as type" list choose "GIF-89a" (or JPG depending upon the type of image). Now choose "Version 89a—Interlaced" (or "Progressive Encoding") from the subtype list on the "Save As…" dialog box. Click "Save." The file appears just like any other, and it is only when it is transmitted that the interlacing occurs.

An alternative to interlaced GIFs or progressive JPEGs is the thumbnail image. A thumbnail is a small version of a much larger and more detailed original image, but because of its compact size, it is able to traverse the Internet comparatively quickly. The thumbnail is linked to the original, larger image. When a visitor clicks the thumbnail, the larger image is downloaded to the browser and displayed in a separate (or sometimes the same) window.

Thumbnails work especially well as a shop window for more detailed goodies contained within. The thumbnailed page is downloaded to the browser quickly, and visitors can choose to view only the larger images they are interested in seeing.

To create a thumbnail, make a duplicate of the original image and use paint editing software, such as Paint Shop Pro or Photoshop, to resize the duplicate. Don't worry about quality, as long as the thumbnail is clear enough to act as a preview for the original image.

PROTECT AND SURVIVE

Ensuring the fruits of your labor are registered with as many search engines as possible is second only to considering download times when designing Web pages. The Internet is a very big place indeed, and the Web sports many millions of sites, all potentially competing with yours for a visitor's browser.

Commercial sites especially are in hot competition with rival sites to capture the attention of surfers with a two-minute attention span. Cool, competent designs and fast download times will help enormously—but only if visitors can find your site in the first place. The trick is to register with as many search engines (such as Yahoo and AltaVista) as possible, each of which sends out Web crawlers to scan sites for information describing their contents. This information is collated and presented to Web users searching for similar sites.

The first step in getting your site noticed is to give it a sensible title—and for "sensible" read "unmissable." This will be picked up by the search engines' Web crawlers. A more subtle ploy is to make sure that all your pictures have what are known as ALT tags.

ALT tags were used in the early days of Web browsers that were unable to display images; Lynx, for example, was (and still is, among those using very old hardware) a very popular text-only browser. An ALT tag is a piece of explanatory text which is displayed in place of an associated picture. Look at the source for an ALT tag, and you will see something like:

```
<IMG
SRC="http://www.wimpleware.co.uk/pics/bobcats.jpg"
ALT="Fabulous Bobcats rockabilly band">
```

Those using browsers unable to display the "bobcats.jpg" image would instead see "Fabulous Bobcats rockabilly band." The ALT tag will also appear if the mouse pointer is moved over the image. You might think that in these

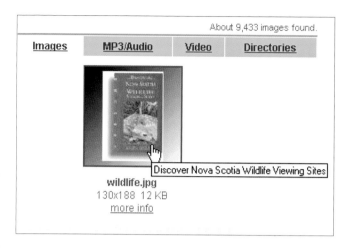

1 | 2
ALT tagging ensures that all-important search-engine listings contain links to your Web pages. They also make navigation easier for those using browsers unable to resolve in-line images.

3
Digimarc offers protection for copyright images by burying an electronic tag deep within the bits and bytes that make up the image.

60

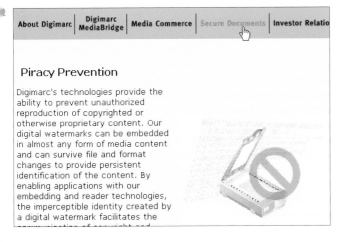

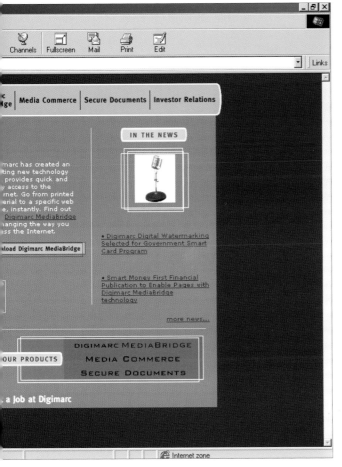

days of powerful browser software there would be no need for ALT tagging, except that a snippet of text can be put to productive use hoodwinking Web crawlers into gathering even more specific text about your site.

ALT tags can also serve as explanations for images designated as links. You might, for example, have a cartoon of someone bailing out of a burning aircraft with an ALT tag saying "Back to home page." Clicking the cartoon takes the visitor back to the main page of the site. And—infrequently, but it does happen—Web users turn off graphics from within their Web browsers to speed surfing. These people will be able to make better sense of your site by viewing ALT tags.

ALT tagging images is easy. Most Web-authoring packages offer tagging as an image-oriented menu option. Adobe's GoLive, for example, offers an "Alt Text" field in which you can type a short sentence after clicking the "Spec" tab of the Image Inspector. Alternatively (though tediously), you can switch your software to a source view and insert an ALT directly into the HTML, as described above. Incidentally, there is no need to ALT tag PNG (portable network graphics) format images, which already contain a text identifier.

Given the globe-spanning, freewheeling nature of the Internet—and especially the Web—it isn't surprising that issues of copyright are hazy. Though copyright exists, just as it does in the "real" world, tracking down someone who has ripped off your copyrighted images isn't going to be easy—how do you prove they are yours in the first place? The answer is digital watermarking. This is a process by which you can add an invisible "marker" to an image, specifying it as your property. Though it will not stop someone from copying it from your site, you can at least prove the image is yours. Point your browser at **www.digimarc.com** for details of utility software that enables you to watermark your own images.

NAVIGATING WITH IMAGE MAPS

Because images are so good at breaking down the language barrier, it makes perfect sense to use them in an active as well as a passive (i.e. pretty) way. Using an image as a tool for navigating your site blends form and function into an unbeatable combination.

There are two methods by which images can be used in this way: you can turn small images into clickable icons, buttons, and the like, which link to a single URL (Uniform Resource Locator), or, for greater impact, you can use a larger detailed picture as an object, called an "image map," which features two or more links.

Each clickable area in the image map is called a "hotspot," and each hotspot can point to an anchor on your main page, to subpages at your site, or to URLs anywhere on the Internet. You can implement an image map as a server-side CGI script (an applet which is run

on the server, rather than downloaded to, and run on, a visitor's computer). Or, you can configure an autonomous map within your Web page, which neatly sidesteps the need for server interaction, either from you or from visitors to your site.

Take care when selecting a suitable image to use as an image map—especially if your map will completely replace other links from your page. The image should lend itself to easy interpretation with lots of visual cues. To this end, you might choose to create a composite picture that has a main image and several obviously clickable supporting images. A map image should contain defined areas suitable to turn into hotspots, and each hotspot should be large enough for visitors to easily access the associated links. It is not a good idea to create a clickable cyberspace keyhole!

1 | 2 | 3

Careful use of images as a tool for navigation —the "image map"— makes viewing a Web site fun. You can use a conventional map featuring clickable hotspots, as in Go's site (1) **www.go-fly.co. uk**, or an image like the Melinamade **www.melinamade. com** map (2), which captures the feel of the site and provides strong visual cues to links. The tree image (3) map on the UCLA site **www.ucla.edu** is echoed throughout the site, giving it the feel of "branching out."

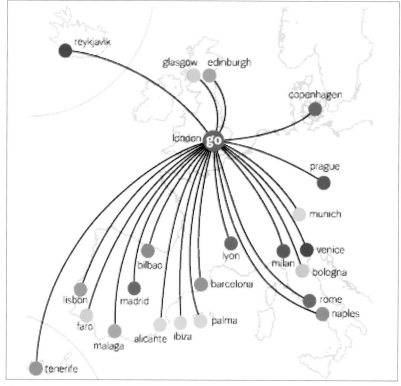

1

2

62

THE BEST ALBUMS OF THE YEAR

4 | 5
A composite image can work just as well as a single image. The Audi image map (4) **www.audi.de** is pure style, blending slick pics with a cool modernist layout. HMV **www.hmv.com** calls up memories of teenage fanzines with a click on your heart-throb image map (5).

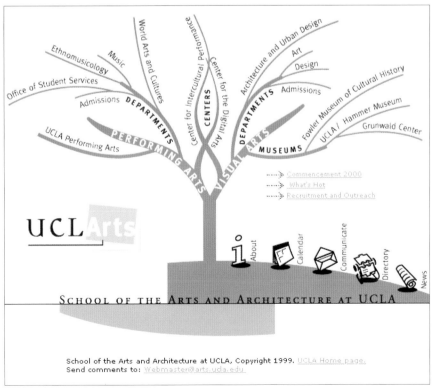

MAKING MAPS

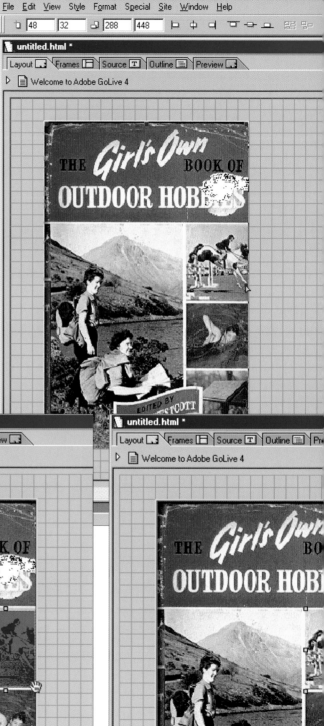

ajor Web-authoring packages, such as FrontPage and GoLive, make it easy to create attractive image maps. GoLive provides an Inspector devoted solely to the task of creating an image map. First, import your chosen image onto a page. Click the image to select it and, from the Image Inspector, click on the "Map" tab. Click the "Use Map" check box to activate the image as an image map. Type a suitable name for the map into the "Map Name" field (or accept the default provided by GoLive), then draw in the first hotspot region by clicking on one of the Region Tools and drawing directly on the image map. Use the grab handles provided to size the newly drawn region until it is just right. You can add a border to the hotspot using the Frame Regions tool.

When the hotspot looks and behaves as you want it to, type a URL into the "Reference" field for whatever it is you want to point at, or use the Browse button to select an object or location. With several hotspots on your image map, use the Pointer tool to select and resize them.

3 | 4
Selecting areas to become "hotspots"— the hyperlinks to other pages…

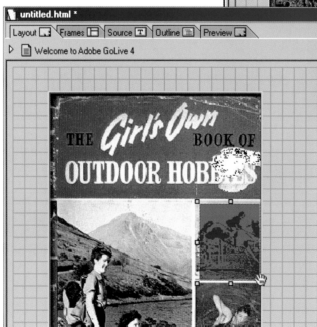

3

4

64

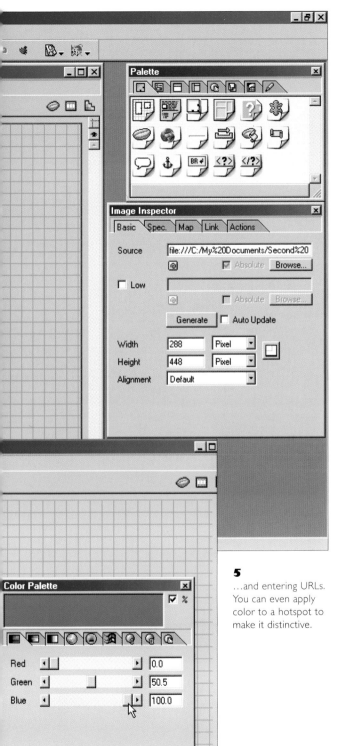

2

1
With Adobe's GoLive authoring software you can create an image map as easily as importing a suitable image.

2
The dialog box shows the different options for creating image maps.

65

5
...and entering URLs. You can even apply color to a hotspot to make it distinctive.

http://www.wimpleware.co.uk/

5

CAUSE AND EFFECTS

Traditional graphic design is all about arranging text and images in a way that is at once functional and aesthetically pleasing. That's true of Web design too, but, unlike design for the printed page, the Web has an extra "multimedia" dimension that will be entirely new to most graphic designers. Sound effects, animated graphics, streaming audio, video clips, marquees, hit counters, and interactive gadgets such as forms, password dialogs, and so on, all are used to great effect on the Web, where the much-heralded multimedia experience has at last found its true home. Technological advances are resulting in ever more powerful and novel ways to use effects that appeal to a sense other than sight.

1

2

1|2|3|4
The opening animation of Paul Smith's **www. paulsmith.co.uk** site is pure funk, with catwalk music and the flavor of the '60s. The left-shifted Union Jack not only provides tension but gives a great space for the animated model to step out from.

5|6|7
The U.K. consumer electronics giant Dixons **www. dixons.com** uses subtle type effects— moving words around in a sentence to change the meaning. This shows how a site doesn't have to be all-embracing to catch the eye: a clever quirk ensures that visitors will remember you.

3

4

5

6

7

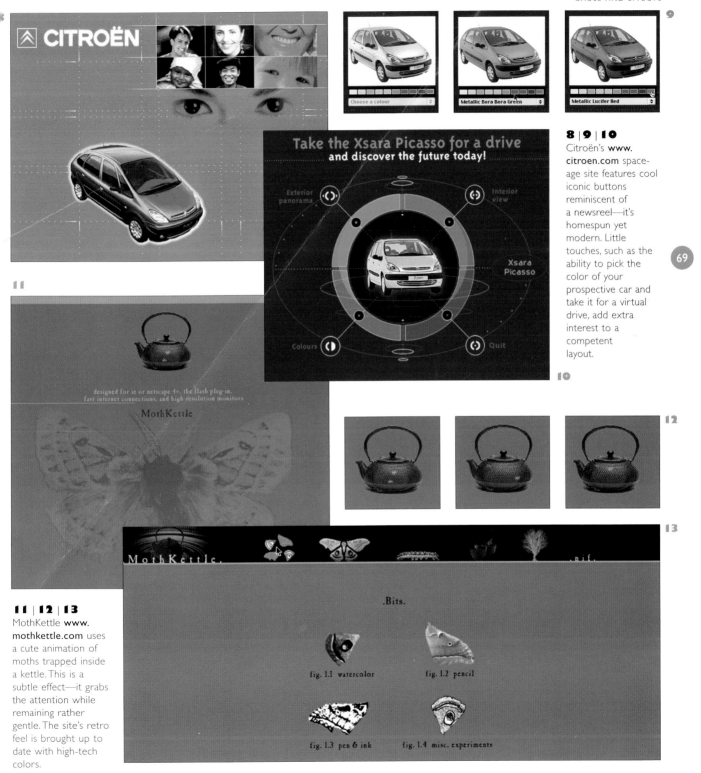

8 | 9 | 10
Citroën's **www. citroen.com** space-age site features cool iconic buttons reminiscent of a newsreel—it's homespun yet modern. Little touches, such as the ability to pick the color of your prospective car and take it for a virtual drive, add extra interest to a competent layout.

11 | 12 | 13
MothKettle **www. mothkettle.com** uses a cute animation of moths trapped inside a kettle. This is a subtle effect—it grabs the attention while remaining rather gentle. The site's retro feel is brought up to date with high-tech colors.

Take the Xsara Picasso for a drive
and discover the future today!

Exterior panorama

Interior view

Colours

Quit

Xsara Picasso

Choose a colour
Metallic Bora Bora Green
Metallic Lucifer Red

designed for ic or netscape 4+, the flash plug-in, fast internet connections, and high-resolution monitors

MothKettle

.Bits.

fig. 1.1 watercolor

fig. 1.2 pencil

fig. 1.3 pen & ink

fig. 1.4 misc. experiments

1

4

6

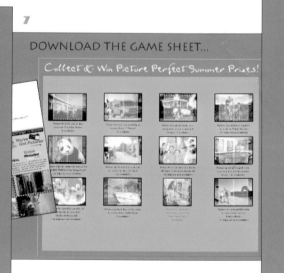

1 | 2 | 3 | 4
5 | 6 | 7 | 8

Kodak's sunny **www. kodak.com** site is ultra-friendly, taking visitors step-by-step through its summer vacation competition. Snappy and quick, it's a joy to watch.

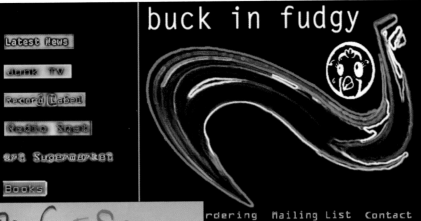

9

9

Buck in Fudgy **www. buckinfudgy.com** uses still-type effects well.

1 0 | 1 1

CyberLive **www. cyberlive.com** demonstrates the overuse of showy effects. (Make up your own mind about the layout.)

71

3

10

PICTURE IT & WIN!
A $250,000 VACATION HOME
OR ONE OF OVER $80 MILLION IN OTHER
PRIZES & DISCOUNTS*

Kodak

World Wide Web

We are your finest source for custom web site designs. Great care is taken to ensure your site is matched to you and your clients needs. We can design everything from an on-line brochure to a full on-line business featuring transactions. As a final touch we can make your site come alive with a wide range of multimedia and scripts.

See our Clients Sites

CyberLive, Inc. ®

34700 Pacific Coast Hwy, #306
Capistrano Beach, CA 92624
Phone: (949) 443-1323
Email: sales@cyberlive.com

Picture It & Win!
50,000 TO BUY YOUR OWN VACATION HOME.

PRIZES   CLOSE WINDOW

8

11

DESIGNING WITH FRAMES

Frames are a way of breaking up into many independent windows an otherwise single scrollable browser window on a single Web page. Using frames, you can fix arbitrary sections of the available browser window space—anchoring a logo, a menu button bar, or an animation in one part of the browser window while making another part available for entirely independent information from an independent Web page.

The power of frames is in the way they demarcate space for a designer, enabling one or more areas ("panes") within the browser window to be fixed, while others act just like nonframed windows. Used carefully, the results can be potent and spectacular and the possibilities for commercial Web site design are enormous.

The downside is that it is all too easy to break up what is already a pretty limited area into even smaller pieces that are confusing, limiting, and, most important of all, ultimately unusable. Frames are comparatively slow to download to a visitor's browser, too, and they're not compatible with every browser—though they are compatible with both Netscape Navigator and Microsoft Internet Explorer.

Many visitors find frames irritating, more so when the visitors are trapped inside a frameset even though they have long since left the portion of the site from which the frames came. The all-important search engine Web crawlers can have a difficult time making sense of framed Web pages also. A Back button may not work as

1 | 2

Framed sites abound on the Web, but viewing them can be a pain as bits of information scroll off the screen and others are squeezed into areas too small to contain them. Browsers unable to display framed sites fall over when encountering one—unless the designer makes provision for them. Eckhart **www. eckhart.nl** makes pleasant and uncluttered use of a framed layout for its on-line interior design shop.

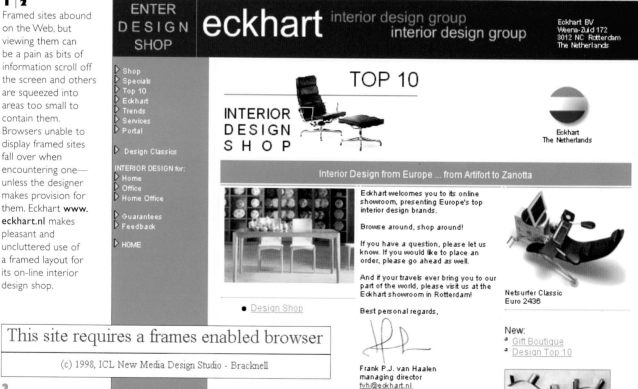

2

3

Used with care, as at Nescafe **www. nescafe.com**, frames demarcate screen areas to great effect.

4

It's easy to create a Web cliché. James Thin **www. jthin.co.uk** uses frames, but they do little to help the layout.

expected and the scroll keys on a visitor's keyboard will work only if they click inside the frame they want to scroll, another irritating "feature."

Of course, the true power of frames lies with you, the designer. It's your responsibility to make sensible use of them, to create pages infinitely stronger than those without frames. Use them carelessly and you'll discover the fastest way to lose visitors.

Netscape is responsible for creating the frame extension to standard HTML, though Microsoft quickly took up the idea. A frame is specified using either a pixel count or as a percentage of overall browser window size (running all the usual risks as a result!) It's a good idea to test your frames-based pages with several browsers to gauge the way they'll look to a visitor.

Frames are available as several types. Basic frames feature a number of border types and color schemes and can be used to delineate screen areas. All browsers that support frames will work with frames of this type. Borderless frames are a variation on the basic frame theme. The latest versions of both Internet Explorer and Netscape Navigator support borderless frames; they can

be used to create aesthetically pleasing screens with separate fixed and scrolling areas.

Microsoft has extended the frame standard to create custom borders and floating frames. A floating frame (also known as an "inline" frame) can be positioned anywhere in the browser window, while normal frames always have at least one edge at the browser's window margin. Inline frames extend the scope for designers, but should be used with care because your pages will be limited to visitors using Internet Explorer.

For those with browsers that don't support frames and for the huge number of visitors who loathe them, it's wise to provide a frame-free version of your pages—available, say, from a home page.

Designers who don't mind dirtying their hands with HTML can include <NOFRAMES> and </NOFRAMES> tags in their framed Web pages. Items between these tags are displayed on browsers incapable of supporting frames.

THE INTERACTIVE WEB 1

Once commercial Web sites were little more than one-way shop windows for whatever it was a company wanted to sell. Now those same companies are creating ever more sophisticated sites, which can gather valuable information about potential customers.

Web sites are increasingly interactive. Many make use of special forms that enable visitors to request product details, brochures, and catalogs, or simply to tell the Web master what they like and don't like about the site. Usually, visitors type their details—name, address, and telephone number—into "fields" on the form, perhaps select from a number of clickable buttons specifying what they want and their impressions of the site, then end by giving their e-mail address and clicking a "submit" button. The data are recorded by the Web site's server and a confirmation is displayed to the visitor.

Why not instead provide an email link for visitors? Sadly, information sent that way is much more difficult to process in such a way that ultimately will be useful. In addition, it is possible to make use of "secure servers" to process sensitive data, such as credit card details, which visitors might not want to send via ordinary e-mail. But perhaps more importantly, it is widely acknowledged that visitors are far more likely to enter their details into an attractive and straightforward form and click on a Submit button, than they are to compose an email message and remember to include all the required information. Computers handle and process raw data with an efficiency and speed that a humanoid can never hope to emulate—so make the most of their abilities by using forms and automated scripting.

As a designer of commercial Web sites, it is very likely that you will be required to design a form at some time. The process is relatively simple, but it pays to understand how forms work and what's going on in the background. Essentially, forms are two-headed beasts with, at their most visible, the actual form into which

1 | 2 | 3
Many commercial sites make use of interactive forms to gather information about the visitors who access them. The simplest form, such as those in place at **www. abbeynational. co.uk, www. egg.com**, and **www. sirius.com**, is one that requests a user name and password to enable you to enter a site, such as a Web mail server.

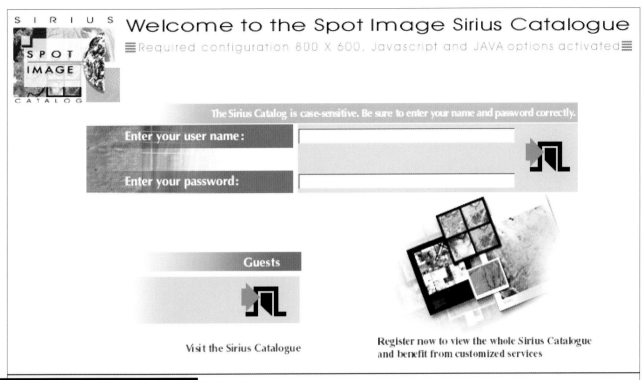

SIRIUS SPOT IMAGE CATALOG

Welcome to the Spot Image Sirius Catalogue

≡Required configuration 800 X 600, Javascript and JAVA options activated≡

The Sirius Catalog is case-sensitive. Be sure to enter your name and password correctly.

Enter your user name:

Enter your password:

Guests

Visit the Sirius Catalogue

Register now to view the whole Sirius Catalogue
and benefit from customized services

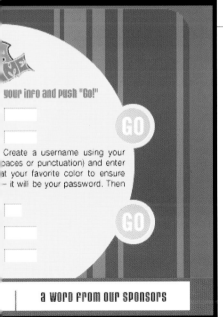

your info and push "Go!"

GO

Create a username using your
[sp]aces or punctuation) and enter
[wh]at your favorite color to ensure
– it will be your password. Then

GO

a word from our sponsors

visitors enter data. Behind the scenes, however, is a computer program known as a "CGI script" (Common Gateway Interface), or simply "script," which is invoked on a special forms server provided by your ISP. When the visitor clicks the Submit button the script is invoked, processes the submitted data, and generates a response of some kind, which is transmitted to the visitor.

For forms to work as they should, your ISP must support CGI scripting. The majority do, and offer ready-made scripts to handle all the usual forms as a "free" service (i.e. included in your subscription). Some offer a bespoke scripting service at a price, while others offer no scripting whatsoever. So the first step to embedding a script in your Web site is to ascertain what, if any, scripting is available from your ISP—e-mail them and ask.

4
Some sites, like **www. kelloggs.com**, dress up their forms to encourage visitors to complete them. Others, like **www. sirius.com** (3), require minimal information—such as user name and password—to be entered before the site can be accessed. The temptation is to fill remaining space with clutter, although restraint, as shown here, is generally the preferred route.

THE INTERACTIVE WEB 2

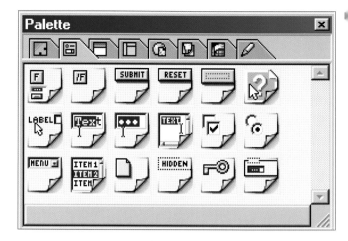

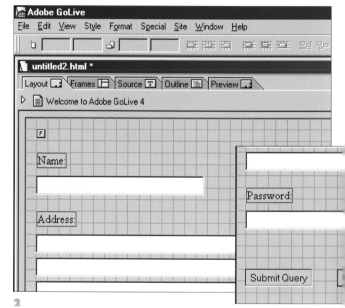

2

Popular Web-authoring packages, such as FrontPage, GoLive, and NetObjects Fusion, provide sample forms that you can use as they are or adapt to your own designs. Some FrontPage forms, however, require that the ISP has FrontPage Server Extensions installed. Other form components and features work only with browsers enabled for HTML 4.0—navigation between fields using the tab key, for example.

Before creating a form, check with your ISP that a script to handle it is available. Most provide scripts for "standard" forms, such as guestbooks, feedback, product ordering, secure servers for sensitive data, and so on. Others readily accept scripts from their clients, but only if they conform to the ISP's requirements.

If your ISP does not provide scripting, it is still possible to use forms, though the results will need a certain amount of manual processing. NetObjects Fusion features forms that use standard e-mail to collate the data entered into them. No interaction with a Web server is required to make use of these forms.

The first step to creating a form with Adobe's GoLive is to select the Basic tab on the Palette, click the Layout Grid tool, and drag it to an open document. Size the resulting layout grid so that it roughly matches your expectations for the form. Although you can simply insert form elements into a free-form document, the results may not be displayed correctly unless the elements are contained within the cells of a table.

Now click on the Forms tab in the Palette, which will display a host of tools to help you create a form (figure 1). Each of the tools has an Inspector linked to it. Select a tool, and the options associated with it are displayed in the relevant Inspector.

Drag a Form tag from the upper left corner of the Palette onto the upper left corner of the layout grid. This tag marks the "beginning" of the form (figure 2). All the elements that will make up your form are contained in

this opening Form tag icon and an associated endform tag icon, which you can drag from the Palette yourself. Or, GoLive will insert it automatically if you choose the Preview view. Use the Form Inspector (figure 3) to specify in the Target field a URL for the CGI script you want to use with the form. With the Inspector, name the form and select an encryption method (if it is going to be used with a secure server).

Click and drag the Label tool to a position on the layout grid and type your field labels, here "name and

76

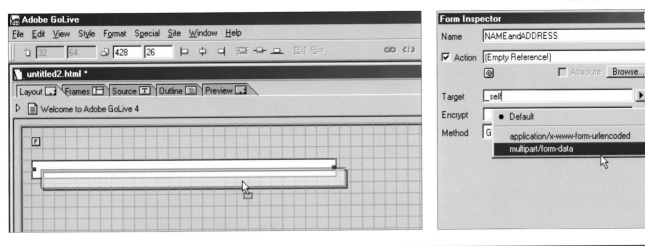

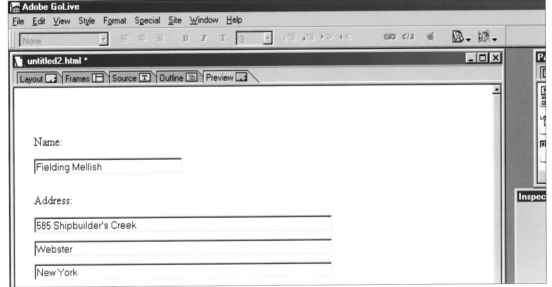

1 | 2 | 3 | 4 | 5 | 6

Adobe GoLive provides a simple way to create forms using point and click techniques and simple draggable tools from the standard Palette and Inspector.

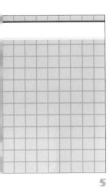

address" (figure 4). Click and drag the Text Area tool and place it just to the right of the name and address label. Use the grab handles to size the Text Area tool until it is big enough to contain a name and address. Use the Submit and Reset tools to add buttons to the form (figure 5). Now switch to Preview mode and view the form in all its glory (figure 6).

Designing attractive and useful forms featuring radio buttons, check boxes, text fields, pop-up lists, and all the other goodies you've seen and used on the Web is

as easy as creating the example outlined above. Each component has a tool that can be dragged from the Palette to the Layout Grid for precise positioning. Each tool has an associated Inspector where you can style it, add encryption, specify external objects such as GIFs in place of the standard button types, and so on.

It is a good idea to validate form data. An easy method is to have a JavaScript downloaded to the visitor's computer. The script checks the form and prompts a visitor if it encounters bad data.

SITE AND SOUND

Though sound will be an unfamiliar medium for many designers, it offers exciting possibilities for enhancing Web pages, creating a stronger overall message and making potentially inaccessible pages available to those who might otherwise miss them, such as the visually impaired.

Sound can be used to create atmosphere, strengthen the impact of an animated logo, and underline a corporate identity (think of Intel's advertising, for example, and you can't help but think of its corporate jingle). Or sound can simply provide spoken information in a way that's instantly familiar and "humanizing" (at least to those who speak the same language).

Speech is subject to the language barrier—even if English is an international language—but sound effects and music can utterly transcend any barriers. You should remember, though, that music can be a double-edged sword. If, for example, you're creating a site for a real-estate company selling off bits of Australia's Ayers Rock, the haunting sound of a didgeridoo might put potential clients in the mood to buy—or remind them that others have a prior claim to the geological formation.

Like graphics, there are any number of formats in which sound clips can be stored and transmitted on the Web. Among the most popular platform-specific formats, wave files can be recognized by their .wav file name extenders. Wave files originate in the PC world, but they work well with Apple Mac browsers too. The Macintosh has its own format known as AIFF (Audio Interchange File Format), though, not surprisingly, it's not as popular. PCs running Windows 9.x can play .aiff files.

Other sound file formats include MIDI files, which are used with synthesizers but can also be played by PC and Macintosh browsers; MPEG, which is also used as a video file format; and the less popular RMF (Rich Music Format).

These formats all have one feature in common: a

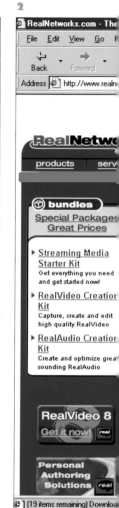

1
RealAudio is a streaming sound technology for which you can download a free player from the RealAudio site.

2
To embed streaming sound in your own Web pages, a sound utility suite, such as the RealNetworks Streaming Media kit, can be downloaded from the Web.

sound clip must be downloaded to the visitor's browser before it can be played. This is fine for a short sound effect but not much good for anything else (unless visitors are prepared to wait—and most aren't!).

RealAudio is a relatively recent technology that gets around the problem of lengthy download times by providing what is known as "streaming audio." This is a method of sending and receiving real-time audio transmissions without the often horrendous wait times. It's a complex process: Briefly, a small amount of audio

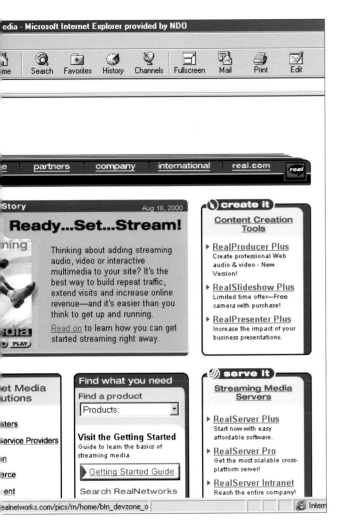

users will be able to make use of embedded audio clips. Both machines have sound hardware and either a built-in mono speaker or add-on stereo speakers. And the latest versions of Microsoft's Internet Explorer and Netscape's Navigator feature support for all the popular digital sound formats. Those they don't support can usually be handled with downloadable plug-ins and helper software. As such, it's always a good idea to provide links to suitable plug-ins whenever you embed multimedia files that might not be handled by standard browser software.

To receive RealAudio transmissions, visitors must install a RealAudio browser plug-in, which is available as a free download from RealAudio's Web site (**www.realaudio.com**). To create streaming sound as part of a Web design, you will need to acquire the authoring software known as RealProducer G2. This can be had from **www.realnetworks.com**.

Creating sound clips is somewhat easier in that your computer is probably already equipped with the software tools necessary. Windows machines have Sound Recorder, a simple utility that records wave format files; and owners of Macs can make use of a bundled application such as SimpleSound, which works in much the same way and produces files in the standard Mac format. Using the resulting clips is a simple matter of making a link to them within a page (or configuring them as an exception to a mouseover or something similar) and uploading the file, along with all other support files, to your server when you go live.

Be aware that copyright exists for sound clips just as it does with images, unless you acquire a clip that specifically states that it's copyright-free. Although there is a big sampling movement that "borrows" excerpts from TV shows, pop music recordings, and so on, unauthorized users could find themselves the subject of litigation.

data—say, 16K—is transmitted to a visitor's browser, where it is buffered. The browser begins to play its reserve buffer of 16K while data continue to be sent and received. Once the initial 16K is received, the process appears to be continuous and live. In practice, streaming audio works very well, unless a big hiccup in data reception interrupts the flow.

Can you always be sure that a visitor's machine is equipped to play sounds? In the new millennium, it seems reasonable to assume that both PC and Mac

STEPS AHEAD

For some, Nike **women.nikejapan.co.jp** is synonymous with style, and the company's logo is seen everywhere. Though Nike's home page is disappointingly (and rather surprisingly) muddled, clicking further into the site rewards the visitor with sleek layouts and contemporary type.

1 2
Colorful clutter (1) fronts an otherwise stylishly simple site (2), which uses stripes of color as navigational aids.

3 4
Animations abound throughout the Nike site. As the mouse pointer passes over the color bars (3), each is highlighted; and when each is clicked, visitors are transported to different footwear ranges. The sneakers pictured right (4) swirl in endless twists and turns as if an emblem of the company's restless energy.

5 **6** **7** **8**
Navigating from the color bars (figure 3, *opposite page*) sets in motion the animated sequence shown here. 'Bliss" begins the series, with fade-up yellow bars, followed by a suggestion of the Olympic rings…

83

9
…eventually reaching a grand finale in the detailed product breakdown depicted right. Simple, strong layout with a sporty theme enhances the Nike message.

ミッドフットサドル
ヒールから中足部にかけてのピ
バックス製ミッドフットサドルが
サポート性を生み出す。

ダイナミックストレッチメッシュ
4方向に伸縮するスパンデックスメッ
シュを採用し、フィット性の向上。

足への衝撃を緩和する
ヒール<エア>を搭載。

アスファルトなどの硬い路面でもソフ
トなクッション力を発揮するデュラロ
ンラバー。最も摩擦の多い、踵外側に
耐久性の高いBRS1000（カーボン配合
ゴム素材）でグリップ力強化。

ALL-AMERICAN DREAM

Coca-Cola **www.cocacola.com** and Levi jeans **www.levi.com** epitomize all that is American in a way no other products ever could. And though the soft drink and work-wear brands are now truly international, both rely on their sassy U.S. roots to sell the dream of a freewheeling, chilled-out (but essentially loving) America to the world's young and their parents. Both sites make heavy use of happy, healthy bodies.

1

1 2 3
Color and shape are used extensively to emphasize Coca-Cola's branding strategy. The site opens with this attractive layout and easy-to-use home page, full of reinforcing images (smiles, athleticism, cuddles, and cash) from which visitors navigate to pages offering added-value desktop wallpapers and screensavers (2,3).

2

3

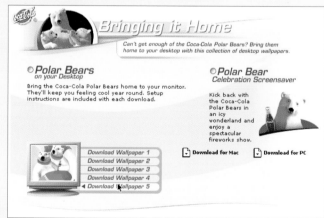

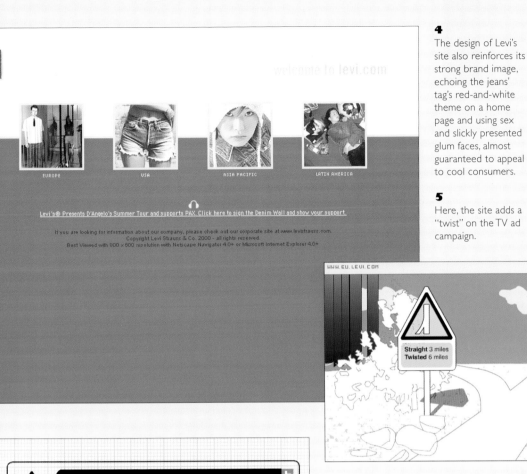

4

The design of Levi's site also reinforces its strong brand image, echoing the jeans' tag's red-and-white theme on a home page and using sex and slickly presented glum faces, almost guaranteed to appeal to cool consumers.

5

Here, the site adds a "twist" on the TV ad campaign.

6 7

Here, Levi's has torn up the traditional single space of the Web page, creating a mosaic of independent windows from which it promotes its "Twisted" jeans brand.

BUBBLE CAR

W hat could be more gentle, attractive, and fun than the humble bubble? Shiny, translucent spheres make the perfect complement for Volkswagen's **www.beetle.de/newversion.htm** new bubble-esque Beetle, providing a sell so soft it's virtually subliminal.

New Beetle
Joy Ride.

Suchen Sie noch Beifahrer für eine New Beetle-Tour durch's Internet? Dann geben Sie doch gleich hier einige Ihrer Interessen an. Der eigens für diesen Zweck installierte Bord-Computer des virtuellen New Beetle sucht passende Mitfahrer für Sie aus. Ist jemand online, der ähnliche Interessen hat, melden wir uns mit einem Chat-Fenster bei Ihnen.

Bin da!

Liebe Dein Auto

Joy Ride

Facts & Figures

Danke!

Feedback

Hilfe

New   Login

1 2
The simple white background sets off the translucent quality of the bubbles, which in turn echo the lines of the car. An arc of bubble buttons leads to greater detail.

3

Bin da!

Liebe Dein Auto

Joy Ride

Facts & Figures

Danke!

Feedback

Hilfe

4

Liebe Dein **Auto**

Darf ich den mal anfassen?
Sie dürfen - aber Vorsicht.
Denn der New Beetle ist
ein Auto zum Verlieben.

Der nächste Frühling
kommt bestimmt. Im New
Beetle!

weiter ...

3 4

Soft curves,
sweeping lines, and
simple pastel colors
continue throughout
the Beetle site,
making its layout
feel very friendly.

5 6

VW thanks you for
visiting, and (right)
well, what would
your ideal Beetle
look like?

5

Danke!

Jerry Hagan

Ryan Hahn

Heacock

Kristian Helm

Aaron Hale

Peter Halliden

Marco Hammerand

Thomas Hanselmann

Nathan Harms

Sarah Harrison

Walid A. Hassan

Marcus Hayden

Gary H. Heinicka

Jon Hemenway

CIRCLES WITHIN CIRCLES

What else would you expect from leading designer Terence Conran but a site **www.conran.co.uk** that leads the field in Web design? This simple layout features a rollover list sporting smart logos from top to bottom. Circles abound, and the contemporary color theme washes over the Web visitor jaded by a thousand RGB (red, green, blue) nightmares.

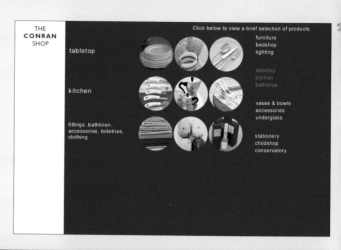

1 2

The circular theme is practical, too, providing a neat way to navigate the Conran empire. Each circular icon opens the door to a different department, be it restaurant, furniture outlet, or fashion store.

3

Sub-pages provide access to greater product detail. Backgrounds are rendered in minimalist gray and use the simplest layouts to great effect.

3

4

CONRAN COLLECTION

CONRAN COLLECTION
12 Conduit Street, London W1R 9TG
Tel: 020 7399 0710, Fax: 020 7399 0711

OPENING HOURS
Monday, Tuesday, Wednesday, Friday and Saturday:
10am-6.30pm, Thursday: 10am-7.30pm, Sunday: 12noon-6pm

PUBLIC TRANSPORT
Underground: Oxford Circus (Bakerloo, Central and Victoria
lines), Piccadilly Circus (Piccadilly and Bakerloo lines)

Manager: Jo Adam

furniture | bedshop | lighting

storage & travel | vases & bowls | underglass

bathshop | kitchen | tabletop

click on a circle to view products

CONRAN COLLECTION
HOME

HOME

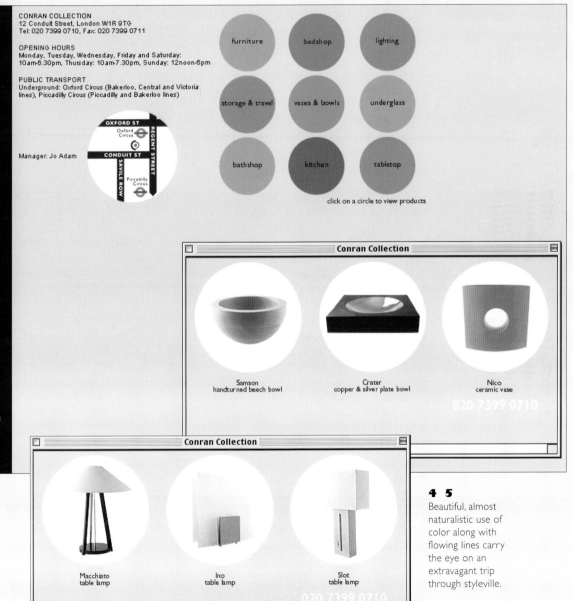

Conran Collection

Samson
handturned beech bowl

Crater
copper & silver plate bowl

Nico
ceramic vase

020 7399 0710

Conran Collection

Macchiato
table lamp

Ino
table lamp

Slot
table lamp

020 7399 0710

4 5
Beautiful, almost
naturalistic use of
color along with
flowing lines carry
the eye on an
extravagant trip
through styleville.

5

LIFESTYLE SELL

Habitat's subtly attractive site could be straight from the pages of a high-quality lifestyle magazine, with its almost textbook approach to layout. Grayscales combine with soft terracotta and complementary blue hues for a look that sidesteps the more usual in-your-face Web page and offers instead a pleasant browse through a coffee-table catalog of the company's products. See it for yourself at **www.habitat.net**.

habitat

La vida
de cada día

Decorar

Jarrones
Lámparas
Alfombras

habitat

En familia o
entre amig

2

1
Sympathetic colors combine for an inspirational haven of home decor ideas— a soothing little oasis that's all your own on the Web.

2 3 4 5
The upper and lower gray bars frame the page, focusing the visitor's attention on the products within.

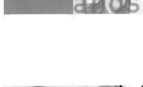

PRIMAVERA VERANO 2000 35 años

In the city una

habitat

5

Subscribe now
Abonnieren Sie
Abónese hoy
Abonnez vous
Habitat Newsletter

3

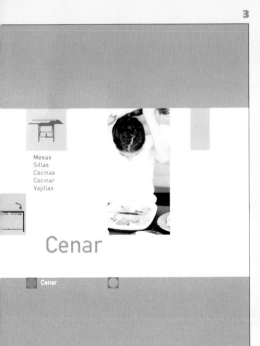

Mesas
Sillas
Cocinas
Cocinar
Vajillas

Cenar

Cenar

4

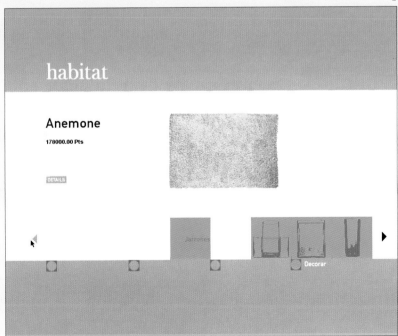

habitat

Anemone

178000.00 Pts

DETAILS

Jarrones

Decorar

91

SNAP, CRACKLE, AND POP

Unlike traditional printed publications, the Web is a truly multimedia experience, offering designers sound and animation to play with as well as images and type. Used sparingly, these added dimensions can elevate Web pages way beyond what is otherwise possible. And, occasionally, you'll come upon a site like that devoted to Snack'Ums **www.snackums.com**, an extravaganza of whirling and twisting animations and scintillating sound effects.

1

4

5

8

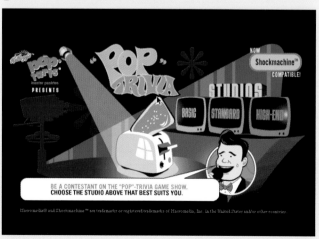

9

1
Sympathetic colors combine for an inspirational haven of home decor ideas— a soothing little oasis that's all your own on the Web.

2 3 4 5
The upper and lower gray bars frame the page, focusing the visitor's attention on the products within.

3

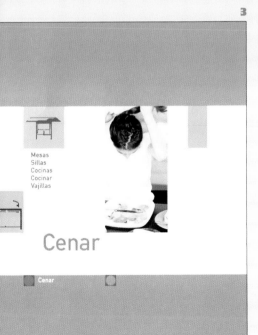

4

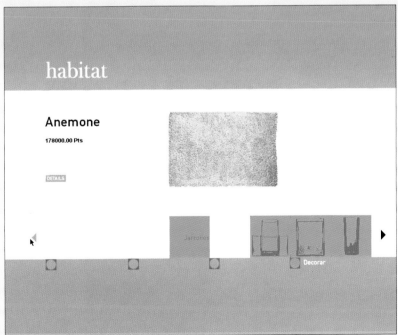

SNAP, CRACKLE, AND POP

Unlike traditional printed publications, the Web is a truly multimedia experience, offering designers sound and animation to play with as well as images and type. Used sparingly, these added dimensions can elevate Web pages way beyond what is otherwise possible. And, occasionally, you'll come upon a site like that devoted to Snack'Ums **www.snackums.com**, an extravaganza of whirling and twisting animations and scintillating sound effects.

1

4

5

8

9

2

3

6

download
tasty
wallpaper

send a
bursting
message

enter
here

7

Sweet stuff that kicks!

OK, so we've given away all our free samples and the sweetstakes is over. That doesn't mean the fun is over. You can still send a bursting message to friends and download cool new wallpaper. Come back soon for more surprises!

Tasty
Downloads!

Send a Friend a
Bursting Message!

Hey

Customize your computer with your favorite Snack'Ums™ baked snacks flavored wallpaper and a NEW hot from the oven custom screensaver.

Blast your buds a supersized surprise with your personalized message hacked in.

Rice
Krispies
Treats
Krunch™

Read our privacy policy. ™, © Kellogg Company. ©2000 Kellogg Company.

10

1 2 3
The Snack'Ums site opens with a deep purple spiral background sporting the product logo and a giant, swirling "Hey."

4 5 6 7
Click on individual Snack'Ums and they explode, showering the screen with fragments and causing yet more of the product to appear and spiral around the background.

8 9 10
Finally, there's a quiz styled as a 1950s-style game show, cleverly capturing visitors' email addresses while innocently providing interactive and added-value entertainment.

PERFORMANCE ART

The gui page **nextdada.luc.ac.be** combines everyday commercial artifacts à la Warhol, such as the bar code and the European "net weight" statement, with smart little Net clichés, like the emoticon-like devil logo, to create a lively and fun layout that works perfectly on the Web and would hold its own on the printed page, too. Arnolfini's angular, hard-edged lines **www.arnolfini.demon.co.uk** are low-tech yet effective—the message is art.

gui

Graphic designer
100% pixelz kungfu & html tai-chi
Grafisch vormgever
100% pure nonsens(e)

A consommer de préfé-rence avant fin : voir capsule. Après ouverture, je ne suis pas responsable pour des malheurs.
Ten minste houdbaar tot einde: zie capsule. Na opening niet meer verant-woordelijk voor gevolgen.
Mindestens haltbar bis Ende : siehe Verschluß-kapsel. Nach dem öffnen nicht mehr Verantwortlich für Ihre Taten.

graphic design •
product design •
webdesign •
multimedia •
graphic user interface •
photography •

Valeur nutritive moyenne par 1000 bytes Gemiddelde voedingswaarde per 1000 bytes Mittlerer Nährwert pro 1000 bytes		
Nextdada	vol.04 [persona non grafika]	9,1
	v.05 [mas-cu-line P 1 X 3 L Z]	2,9
Notre Maison / Ons Huis / Our House		12,7 Mb
Histoires de voyage / Reisverhalen / Travelogues		15,4 Mb
La Vie en Rose / Het Leven / Life		16,8 Mb

"E-MAIL"

Poids net
Netto gewicht
Nettogewicht
72kg ℮

[CONT. ON NEXT PAGE]

2

ARNOLFINI

Visual Arts
Performance
Cinema
Dance
Music
Education
Bookshop
Cafe/Bar

3

4

1 2
The knocked-back duotone bodies in the background remain almost unseen— abstract even— adding layered depth to the bold layout.

3 4 5 6
Arnolfini's stark black home page belies a site that becomes increasingly disappointing as you navigate its sub-pages.

ARNOLFINI LIVE

Arnolfini Live presents some of the most innovative and exciting performance companies working today.

Thursday 1st to Sunday 4th June Gallery Installation on display until 11 June	**Reckless Sleepers** *Breaking Symmetry*
Friday 9th and Saturday 10th June 8.00pm	**Charlie Morrissey** *Line*
Friday 16 to Monday 20 June opening times vary - see listing for full details	**Blast Theory** *Desert Rain*
Saturday 17 June 8.00pm	**Forced Entertainment** *Emanuelle Enchanted*

Shattered Anatomies
Traces of the Body in Performance

Edited by Adrian Heathfield with Fiona Templeton and Andrew Quick Designed by Lewis Nicholson Produced by Formation

General Information . Visual Arts . Performance . Dance . Cinema .
Music . Education . Bookshop . Publications . Cafe/Bar . Friends . Links

ARNOLFINI

ARNOLFINI
ARNOLFINI PUBLICATIONS
NEW TITLES
AND UPDATED STOCK LIST
1976 - 1998

INTRODUCTION

PAINTING & DRAWING

SCULPTURE

MIXED MEDIA & INSTALLATION

PHOTOGRAPHY

EDUCATION

LIVE ART

ARNOLFINI PUBLICATIONS

5

ARNOLFINI
Music

FrontRunners contemporary jazz and new music

Saturday 11 March 8.00pm
David Jean-Baptiste Special Quintet

In this new and genuinely special meeting, clarinettist David Jean-Baptiste, most recently heard at Arnolfini with David Murray's UK Posse, brings two of the USA's brightest younger generation jazz stars to Britain. Acclaimed for his recordings with his own Fo'tet and a major contributor to bands led by David Murray and Michael Brecker, breathtaking drummer Ralph Peterson Jnr is a fine match for the stylistic scope and brilliance that saxophonist James Carter brings to his understanding of the entire Black American tradition. Jean-Baptiste adds fellow first division Londoners Zoe Rahman (piano) and Ricardo dos Santos (double bass) to this unique quintet.
Tickets £8.00/£6.00 concessions

Monday 27 March 8.00pm
Eberhard Weber

Last seen in Bristol in 1995 and more recently on the main stage at Bath Festival, Eberhard Weber, bass-player extraordinaire and long-time sideman with Jan Garbarek's group, plays a stunning solo bass set. Weaving a rich tapestry of rhythmically structured sound planes (played on his own custom-designed electric bass through a number of subtly operated 'live' electronic devices) he creates dream-like pieces of beautiful and haunting melodies.
Tickets £8.00/£6.00 concessions

6

HIGH-TECH SHOPPING

Computer-literate companies don't always manage to create competent Web designs, but both Iomega www.iomega.com and Apple www.apple.com are among the better of the high-tech sites. Both use clean, crisp white backgrounds and variations on their products to create navigable image maps.

1 2 3
The colorful header bar anchors the layout. The Iomega removable media products make for interesting high-tech rollovers.

4 5 6
Apple's clickable tabs—so like those featured on index cards—accentuate the company's no-nonsense (yet fun) approach to selling computers. The iMac colors (or "flavors") are continued in the stylish buttons.

Apple

The new PowerBook. Make desktop movies anywhere.

iBook. Black Tie Optional.

Hot News Headlines   Market Research Shows Apple is Still #1 for Education

Store   iReview   iTools   iCards   QuickTime   Support

Create your account   View Current Order   Education   Worldwide   Help

Step 1: Take your pick (they all taste good)

▶ Click on a flavour.

iMac   iMac DV   iMac DV *Special Edition*

£1,199 inc VAT   Graphite

400MHz G3 Processor, 128MB Memory, 56K Modem, 13GB disk storage, dual 400 Mbps FireWire ports, video editing software, slot loading DVD drive, stereo speakers by Harman Kardon, dual USB Ports, 10/100 Mbps Ethernet.

Includes iMovie, Appleworks, Internet Explorer, 3D games and more.

Tangerine
Strawberry
Blueberry
Grape
Lime

Hz G3 Processor, 64MB ry, 56K Modem, 10GB torage, dual 400 Mbps re ports, video editing re, slot loading DVD stereo speakers by n Kardon, dual USB 10/100 Mbps Ethernet.

s iMovie, Appleworks, t Explorer, 3D games re.

Store   iReview   iTools   iCards   QuickTime   Support
Create your account   View Current Order   Education   Worldwide   Help

Step 2: Select memory for your iMac.

▶ Choose an amount of memory based on your needs.

Summary
- DVD-ROM drive
- Graphite
- Accessory kit
- 13GB IDE drive
- 15" Display built-in
- 56K internal modem
- iMac DV 400MHz Special Edition
- 10/100BASE-T Ethernet
- Two FireWire ports
- VGA video mirroring
- Keyboard

○ Learn More

128 MB
Allows you to run more applications at once and improves performance.
Save 64MB when you select 192MB or more with a HP printer.
Select

192 MB
Provides the power to create complex graphics and speed up 3D games.
Select

256 MB
Enables challenging processing such as video and graphics editing.
Select

97

BODY BEAUTIFUL

The Web is now out of the exclusive hands of academics and the military and firmly in the hands of the people—a fact confirmed by sites such as that of the Body Shop **www.the-body-shop.com**. There are warm colors, smiley faces, soft-focus logos, and layouts that wouldn't look out of place in women's magazines. Each page unfurls to enable visitors to delve into the feature-like items within.

Welco
to T

Select Th

2

1

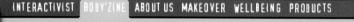

INTERACTIVIST BODY'ZINE ABOUT US MAKEOVER WELLBEING PRODUCTS   K

[Inspiration]

BODY'ZINE

The hunger for youth everlasting never ended particularly happily in fairy tales. "She", H Rider Haggard's African queen was consumed by fire; Countess Elizabeth, the Transylvanian who bathed in virgin's blood, came to a sticky end; and everything went pear-shape for Dorian Gray. How much better to be reconciled to the passage of time, to accept and enjoy each stage of life as an opportunity for experiment and adventure.

Anita Roddick

NAKED BODY

How old is old?

How different is a five-year-old's view of the world from that of an 83-year-old?

Feel happy

Simple stuff you can do to feel happy.

Breeding disaster

Once upon a time evolution was a natural process but now advances in genetic engineering mean that we can modify food and, one day, even a child. But are we right to force the pace of change?

4

IS

What's
justice f
oil comp
species
domesti
is our be

We enc
importa
individu
politics
self-este
valid an

the

I PLC.

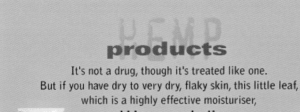

products

It's not a drug, though it's treated like one.
But if you have dry to very dry, flaky skin, this little leaf,
which is a highly effective moisturiser,
could be your salvation...

Hand Protection
hard-core care for
hard-working hands

Soap
all cleansing,
no drying

Elbow Grease
get tough with
dryness

Well Oiled
max lubrication for
bath, body and
back rubs

Lip Conditioner
lip care that
can't be licked

...dy Shop

that's right for you...

...SA   CANADA

[Principles]

...re company doing fighting for
...tribe against a multi-national
...for the survival of endangered
...e British Government on
...nswer's simple. Campaigning
...s selling skin and hair care.

...ake their own stand for what is
...ept the power they have both
...ly. And to use that power. The
...no more than an expression of
...ccept that our opinions are
...ght to be heard.

HUMAN RIGHTS AWARD
This year The Body Shop launches
international human rights award
recognising inspiration in the face
adversity.

...n rights award

INTERACTIVIST BODY'ZINE ABOUT US MAKEOVER WELLBEING PRODUCTS   HOME

welcome to the
virtual make-over

Inside, you will learn how to create the latest
great looks in our make-up master-class.
Alternatively you can select a model and create
your own looks using the Colourings range.

START

This application has been developed to be genuinely useful as well as
great fun to use. As a result, the high image-quality employed means
that you may need to wait for a minute or two for it to download
(dependant on the type of computer and internet connection that you
have).

You'll need the Flash 3 plug-in, so if you don't already have it installed
you can download it for free.

GET
FLASH

Approx. 200k

Copyright © 1999 The Body Shop International PLC.
Copyright courtesy of Peartree Music 'Bowl of Plums' CD - Piers Partidge
Click here for legal restrictions and terms of use applicable to this site.

1 2 3 4 5
The Body Shop has
chosen colors that
reflect contemporary
interest in things
ethnic. Layouts are
unremarkable yet
appealing. Though
you'd be forgiven for
assuming that each
page is from a
different site, The
Body Shop holds its
pages together with a
homespun 1950s
charm that is at once
familiar and
welcoming.

ART FORM

The Artnet site **www.artnet.com** is a fine-art oriented search engine that directs visitors to items of art for sale and to current exhibitions. The designer's task here is to make the page functional yet attractive. Though heavy use is made of classic underlined hyperlinks, they are combined with enough fine art (such as the Arbus photograph and the Neel picture) to create an engaging and practical Web site.

1

1 2

Artnet features a search field located in a banner at the top of the page. A series of buttons provides access to added-value features, such as the on-line magazine.

artnet.com®

THE ART SEARCH ENGINE   [search]

site map   member services   resources   about us   investor relations

home | galleries | artists | auctions | printstore | bookstore | magazine | sign-in/up

new
African Art Auctions Database
click here for a free trial

GROVE **art**   new
Grove Dictionary of Art
click here to explore

IN AUCTIONS:

Diane Arbus
Two Girls in Matching Bathing Suits, Coney Island
1967
gelatin silver print
14 x 14 in.
Est. 6,000-8,000 USD.

ONLINE AUCTIONS

American Dream
june 28 - july 13
click here to view auctions

FEATURED GALLERY:

Vered Gallery, East Hampton
Claes Oldenburg, *Fag End Study,* 1975

NEW GALLERIES:

FINE ART:
Gallery Alina, Framingham.
Gallery Paule Anglim, San Francisco.
Art Advisor Services/Juan Calero
Saldivar, Mexico City.
The Attic Gallery, Portland.
Beaux Arts, London.
Belloc-Lowndes Fine Art, Inc., Chicago.
Bellwether Gallery, Brooklyn.
John Berggruen Gallery, San Francisco.
Bernier/Blades Gallery, Athens.
Galerie Simon Blais, Montreal.
Galerie Louis Carré & Cie, Paris.
Center for Figurative Painting, New York
Chisholm Gallery, Wellington.
Monte Clark Gallery, Vancouver.
Galeria Thomas Cohn, São Paulo.
Conner Contemporary Art, Washington, D.C.
Contemporary Fine Arts, Berlin-Mitte.
Coskun & Co. Fine Art, London.
Leslie Feely Fine Art, New York.
Feichtner & Mizrahi Gallery, Vienna.
Rijnaut & Paol Fine Art, Amsterdam.
Goya-Girl Press, Inc., Baltimore.
Hackett-Freedman Gallery, San Francisco.
Charlton Hall Galleries, Inc., Columbia.
Richard Heller Gallery, Santa Monica.

ALICE NEEL

FEATURED BOOK:

Alice Neel
Exhibition Catalogue
Published to accompany the first major exhibition of her work since 1974, now opening at the Whitney Museum of American Art.

NEW RELEASES:
Art31|Basel Catalogue for the world's leading modern and contemporary art fair. An indispensible guide to today's art market.

The Prints of Roy Lichtenstein: A Catalogue Raisonné 1948-1993 Mint copies in extremely limited quantities.

Tyler Graphics: Catalogue Raisonné, 1974-1985 Rare copies of this invaluable resource.

Yves Klein: Descriptive Catalogue of Editions and Sculptures Beautifully produced catalogue raisonné from Guy Pieters.

The Art of Dan Namingha Limited

IN ARTNET
MAGAZINE

Barbara Kruger, *Untitled,* 1994, now appearing in "Barbara Kruger" at the Whitney Museum of American Art

NEW THIS MONTH IN U.S. MUSEUMS
Wonderland, Van Gogh, Barbara Kruger, athletic shoes, Sol LeWitt, Georgia O'Keeffe, more.

GHOST ARCHITECTURE
by Hunter Drohojowska-Philp 5/31/00
The uncanny photos of James Casebere.

Nordstern
ART
Sponsored by AXA Nordstern Art Insurance Corporation.

ASK MARK KOSTABI
by Mark Kostabi 6/14/00
Questions and answers with *Artnet Magazine*'s own advice columnist.

BE GNOMES
by Charlie Finch 6/30/00
Creating souls for the third millennial machines.

artnet.com

home | gallerie

categories
MODERN
CONTEMPORARY
PHOTOGRAPHY
AMERICAN
20TH CENTURY
DECORATIVE ARTS

artists index

theme auctions
AMERICAN DREAM
FLOWERS
BY CHAGALL

services
BIDDER
REGISTRATION
MY ACCOUNT
HOW TO CONSIGN

information
FAQ
AUCTION RESULTS
TESTIMONIALS
COLLECTORS
COLUMN

Winning B
Name
Runners
Name

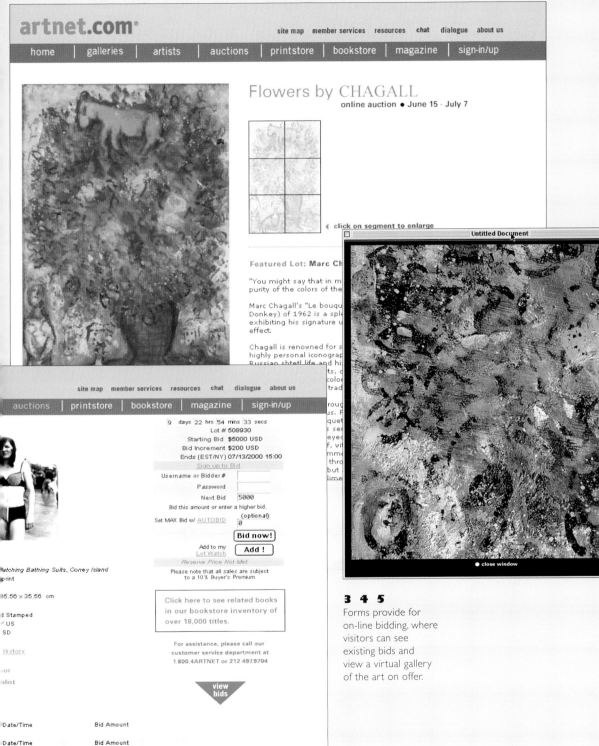

artnet.com®

site map · member services · resources · chat · dialogue · about us

home | galleries | artists | auctions | printstore | bookstore | magazine | sign-in/up

Flowers by CHAGALL
online auction ● June 15 - July 7

◄ click on segment to enlarge

Featured Lot: Marc Ch

"You might say that in m
purity of the colors of the

Marc Chagall's "Le bouqu
Donkey) of 1962 is a spl
exhibiting his signature u
effect.

Chagall is renowned for s
highly personal iconograp
Russian shtetl life and hi

Untitled Document

● close window

site map · member services · resources · chat · dialogue · about us

auctions | printstore | bookstore | magazine | sign-in/up

9 days 22 hrs 54 mins 33 secs
Lot # 508930
Starting Bid $5000 USD
Bid Increment $200 USD
Ends (EST/NY) 07/13/2000 15:00
Sign up to Bid
Username or Bidder #
Password
Next Bid 5000
Bid this amount or enter a higher bid.
Set MAX Bid w/ AUTOBID   (optional)
0

Bid now!

Add to my
Lot Watch   **Add !**

Reserve Price Not Met
Please note that all sales are subject
to a 10% Buyer's Premium

Click here to see related books
in our bookstore inventory of
over 18,000 titles.

For assistance, please call our
customer service department at
1.800.4ARTNET or 212.497.9704

**view
bids**

atching Bathing Suits, Coney Island
print

35.56 x 35.56 cm

d Stamped
US
SD

History

or
alist

Date/Time   Bid Amount

Date/Time   Bid Amount

3 4 5
Forms provide for
on-line bidding, where
visitors can see
existing bids and
view a virtual gallery
of the art on offer.

THE DARK SIDE

Echoes of the stark designs of the 1930s minimalist Bauhaus school pervade BMW's Web pages **www.bmwgroup.com**. The Bavarian motor company's monochrome slickness sells cars to image-conscious baby boomers with money to burn, while the Bauhaus Museum Web site **www.bauhaus.de** provides BMW with back-up inspiration.

Bauhaus–Archiv/Museum für Gestaltung

1 2
The Bauhaus Museum home page cycles colors set against a series of square, monochrome buttons that are used to navigate it.

3 4 5
Pay the Bauhaus Museum a virtual visit via this interactive tour.

BMW Group

Home | Die BMW Group | **Investor Relations** | Karriere | News & Information | Engagement | Veranstaltungen | Innovation

Geschäftsbericht 1999.
BMW Group beschließt
Neuorientierung.

▸ Übersicht
Alle Grafiken und Tabellen
Alle PDF-Downloads
BMW Group in Zahlen

▸ Vorwort des
Vorstandsvorsitzenden
Bericht des Aufsichtsrats
BMW Group Lagebericht
BMW Aktie
BMW Group
Jahresabschluss

6 7
BMW relies on the
arrogance of its
company architecture
(6) to provide the
authority necessary
to sell automobiles.
The rule of thirds
applies throughout,
though BMW has
animated the
autobahn in the
banner (7).

103

7

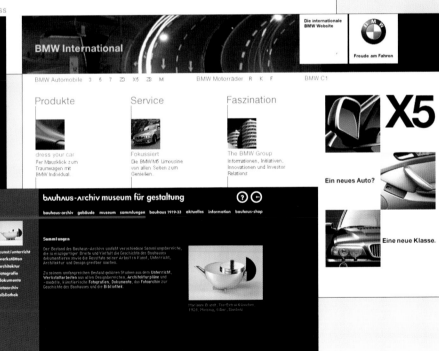

‑33 **aktuelles information bauhaus-shop**

rchiv / Museum für Gestaltung
ferstraße 14
5 Berlin (Tiergarten)

ist täglich, außer dienstags, von 10.00 –
geöffnet.

s‑Archiv zeigt in einer ständigen
usstellung Ausschnitte seiner Sammlung.
Sonderausstellungen präsentieren einzelne
er aktuelle Themenbereiche aus Kunst,
und Design der Moderne.

st es möglich Informationen zum Bestand der
chiv‑Bibliothek über den neuen
katalog zu erhalten.

**Die internationale
BMW Website**

Freude am Fahren

BMW International

BMW Automobile 3 5 Z3 X5 Z8 M   BMW Motorräder R K F   BMW C1

Produkte

dress your car
Per Mausklick zum
Traumwagen mit
BMW Individual

Service

Fokussiert
Die BMW M5 Limousine
von allen Seiten zum
Genießen

Faszination

The BMW Group
Informationen, Initiativen,
Innovationen und Investor
Relations

X5

Ein neues Auto?

Eine neue Klasse.

bauhaus-archiv museum für gestaltung
bauhaus-archiv gebäude museum sammlungen bauhaus 1919-33 aktuelles information bauhaus-shop

kunst/unterricht
werkstätten
architektur
fotografie
dokumente
fotoarchiv
bibliothek

Sammlungen

Der Bestand des Bauhaus-Archivs umfaßt verschiedene Sammlungsbereiche,
die in einzigartiger Breite und Vielfalt die Geschichte des Bauhauses
dokumentieren sowie die Resultate seiner Arbeit in Kunst, Unterricht,
Architektur und Design greifbar machen.

Zu seinem umfangreichen Bestand gehören Studien aus dem Unterricht,
Werkstattarbeiten aus allen Designbereichen, Architekturpläne und
-modelle, künstlerische Fotografien, Dokumente, das Fotoarchiv zur
Geschichte des Bauhauses und die Bibliothek.

Marianne Brandt, Tee-Extrakännchen,
1924, Messing, Silber, Ebenholz

5

VIEW DATA

The San Francisco Museum of Modern Art Web site www.sfmoma.org relies on strong branding, interesting JavaScripts, and sensible organization to rise above its workmanlike layout. Isolate the elements on the page and you're left with little to convince, yet the overall feel of the site is contemporary and satisfying. Otherwise dull details of opening times and the like are made to appear desperately necessary and interesting.

1 2 3 4

At the San Francisco Museum of Modern Art site, strong use of color coordinates subject or content areas such as opening times. Chic graphics and consistent use of banners reinforce company identity throughout.

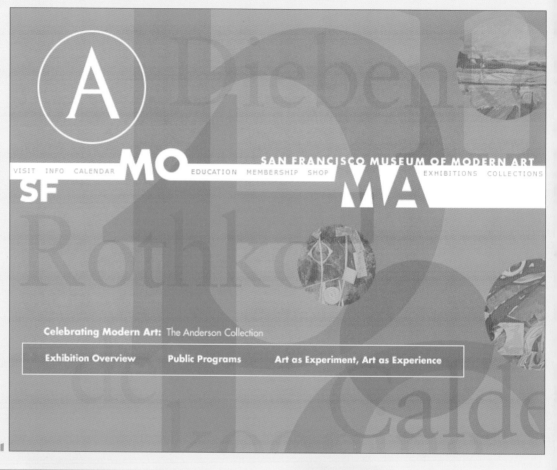

SF MO MA

VISIT INFO CALENDAR   EDUCATION MEMBERSHIP SHOP   EXHIBITIONS COLLECTIONS E•SPACE

SEARCH >   SFMOMA

VISITOR INFORMATION

+ map LOCATION

San Francisco Museum of Modern Art
151 Third Street (between Mission and Howard Streets)
San Francisco, CA 94103

Telephone: 415.357.4000
TDD: 415.357.4154
Fax: 415.357.4037

HOURS
SFMOMA is open on Mondays and closed on Wednesdays.

Gallery Hours
Open every day (except Wednesdays) 11 a.m. - 6 p.m.
Summer hours (Memorial Day - Labor Day) 10 a.m. - 6 p.m.
Open late Thursdays until 9 p.m.

Please note that exhibition galleries close 15 minutes prior to the closure of the
Museum.

The Museum is closed on Wednesdays and on the following public holidays:
Fourth of July, Thanksgiving, Christmas, New Year's Day

New Balance
Cushioning (detail)
1999
Collection New Balance Athletic Shoe,

COLLECTIONS : OVERVIEW

RECENT ACQUISITIONS   ARCHITECTURE+DESIGN   PHOTOGRAPHY

PAINTING+SCULPTURE   MEDIA ARTS

1. Robert Motherwell *Elegy to the Spanish Republic, No. 57*
2. Robert Rauschenberg *Collection (Hoarfrost Editions), 1962-*
3. T.L. Pflueger *Best Love View Renderings of the Projected*
4. Dan Graham *Opposing Mirrors and Video Monitors on Time D*
5. John Gutmann *Memory, 1939*

VISIT INFO CALENDAR   EDUCATION MEMBERSHIP SHOP   EXHIBITIONS COLLECTIONS E•SPACE

SF MO MA

SEARCH >   SFMOMA

5

The Louvre **www. louvre.fr**, too, uses color effectively to identify themes. The site also boasts a "virtual tour."

5

LOUVRE   **Visite virtuelle** Peintures   Sommaire

Palais et musée
– Histoire du Louvre
– Collections
– Visite virtuelle
– Actualité

Activités
– Expositions
  temporaires
– Auditorium
– Visites-conférences
  et ateliers

Informations
– Mode d'emploi
– Boîtes aux lettres
– Publications et
  bases de données

– Vente de billets
– Louvre.edu
– Boutique électronique

Ces pages vous
sont présentées
grâce à Shiseido

Deuxième moitié du XVIIe siècle
Hollande

ON THE ROAD

What else to sell off-road and leisure vehicles than earthy colors, rugged layouts, and all-action shots of the cars being put through their paces? Jeep's site **www.jeepunpaved.com** steers the great outdoors indoors, while Nissan's **www.nissan.com** also uses color to emphasize an association with things green.

1

2

The Jeep vehicle lineup for 2001 includes the legendary Jeep Wrangler, the adventuresome Jeep Cherokee and the technologically refined Jeep Grand Cherokee.

1 2

With its excellent use of rollover graphics, **www.jeepunpaved.com** is indeed "adventuresome" and "technologically refined."

3

3

Earth covers and "ragged" frames reinforce the ultimate purpose of the four-wheel drive vehicles (even though few will venture further than the supermarket parking lot).

4

Rustad femma och tvåa i STCC på Knutstorp söndag 28:e maj.

NYA **MAXIMA V6**

NYA **PATROL GR**

NYA **ALMERA**

KÖP NY NISSAN

4
Nissan goes for
a slightly more
traditional layout,
with an action shot
of the car glinting in
low sunlight and links
to product details
down the left-hand
margin.

5

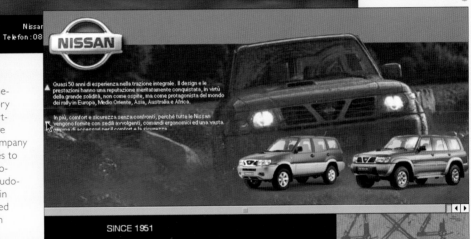

Quasi 50 anni di esperienza nella trazione integrale. Il design e le
prestazioni hanno una reputazione meritatamente conquistata, in virtù
della grande solidità, non come ospite, ma come protagonista del mondo
dei rally in Europa, Medio Oriente, Asia, Australia e Africa.

In più, comfort e sicurezza senza confronti, perché tutte le Nissan
vengono fornite con sedili avvolgenti, comandi ergonomici ed una vasta
gamma di accessori per il comfort e la sicurezza.

SINCE 1951

4×4

5 6 7
Sepia-toned time-
lines tell the story
of Nissan's sport-
utility and leisure
vehicles. The company
uses green tones to
underline its eco-
friendliness. Pseudo-
blueprints fade in
from an animated
sequence, which
contrasts old
and new.

MILJÖPOLICY NISSAN SVERIGE AB

Miljödeklarationer för
samtliga Nissan modeller.
(pdf-format)

MICRA

ALMERA

PRIMERA

MAXIMA QX

TERRANO II

PATROL GR

KING CAB

SERENA CARGO

NISSAN **MILJÖ**

MODELLPROGRAM

6

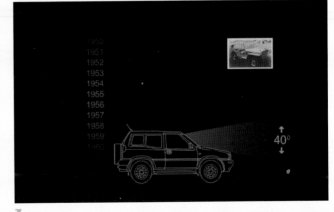

1950
1951
1952
1953
1954
1955
1956
1957
1958
1959
1960

40°

7

OBJECTS OF DESIRE

The Museum of Modern Art **www.moma.org**, lighter manufacturer Zippo **www.zippo.com**, and Alessi **www.alessi.com** use cutouts of objects set against simple backgrounds as basic units of design. On the Zippo page (shown right), the spotlight is on the flame and the fiery orange type, as they flicker across the moody, black backdrop.

Keeper
of the Flame
2000 Collectible of the Year

© 2000 Zippo Manufacturing Company • Please read the Legal Notice

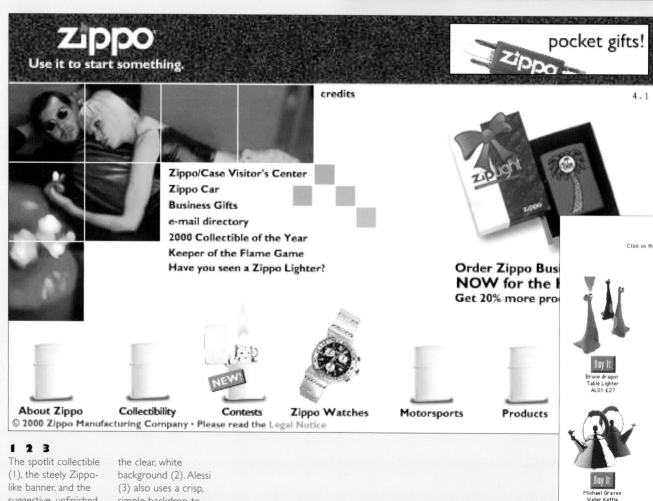

1 2 3
The spotlit collectible (1), the steely Zippo-like banner, and the suggestive, unfinished puzzle make for a striking contrast with the clear, white background (2). Alessi (3) also uses a crisp, simple backdrop to striking effect.

MoMA
online store

4 5 6
When presented against the almost bare backgrounds, images from the Museum of Modern Art create a surreal design that is novel and eye-catching.

Send a MoMA E-Card   What's New   MoMA S

MoMA.org
The Museum of Modern Art

What's On Now   **Collection**   **Educational Resources**   **Visit the Museum**   **Join MoMA**   **The MoMA Online Store**

■ **Current Exhibitions**
Making Choices
Modern Living

■ **The MoMA Online Store**

 Introducing the MoMA Swatch

 Now available: Making Choices exhibition catalogue.

Dream Factory

online store for full product discriptions and to place orders.

Buy It
Magic Bunny
Toothpick Holder
ALS3 £16

Buy It
Alessi
Sugar Sifter
ALS4 £10

Buy It
Alessi
Butter Dish
ALS7 £15

Buy It
Alessi
Firebird
ALS8 £33

eedb

◢ **MoMA menu**   Browse | Gift Ideas | Search   ▷ | Personal Accounts | Help

Browse by [Category ▼]

You can review our collection of products and personalize your browsing:
by selecting a category of products
by choosing all products made by a particular designer

 Books & CD's

 Exhibition Related Products

 Kitchen

 On Sale Now

 Children

 Fashion Accessories

 Lighting

 Tabletop

 Desk Accessories & Stationery

 Furniture & Accessories

 Membership

POWER PLAY

Soap opera started with radio advertising in the 1930s and was still being used to sell coffee half a century later. On the Web, even electricity companies, such as npower **www.npower.com,** make use of high drama to play off against the worries of Web surfers. The layout here is utterly simple, relying on a slide show to add and sustain interest. Multimedia adds new dimensions to what we think of as layout.

1

4

5

8

9

2

**Can't sleep dear?
What's wrong?**

3

6

Is it me?

7

10

OK, so worrying about your electricity supplier
isn't the most important thing in life,
but you do have a choice.

That's why at npower we're working
to lower your bills.

1 2
A straightforward
message simply
presented sucks you
into the nightmare
world of worrying
about electricity
suppliers.

**3 4 5 6 7
8 9**
Stark black
backgrounds with
fade-in Flash-powered
text and graphics
effects build to the
punchline.

10
A final frame that
switches to a
friendlier red-out-of-
white color theme
underlines the point.

WOULD YOU CREDIT IT?

Time and again, crisp white backgrounds prove their worth on the Web. Goldfish **www.goldfish.com**, Marbles **www.marbles.com,** and Mastercard **www.mastercard.com** show that traditional layouts set against white backdrops are the way to create eye-catching and satisfying Web sites that look instantly familiar and enormously friendly.

2

112

get **marbles**™ low interest rate (4.5% APR)*

get a free CD
find out more
details
application status
my account

help

marbles card is issued by HFC Bank plc and is only available to persons aged 21 or over, who are resident in the U.K. or Channel Islands, subject to status and conditions.

marbles has no annual fee. *APR 4.5% on Transactions and Balance Transfers fixed for 6 months from account opening after which this [...] which applies at that time (currently APR 14.9%). A handling fee of 1.5% (minimum of [...] Balance Transfers: APR 16.7% for Cash Advances other than Balance Transfers [...] and APRs are variable. No interest on Transactions if the balance is paid in full by [...] Transaction. Interest payable on Balance Transfers and other Cash Advances from [...] is 3% of the outstanding balance, with a minimum of £5 or the balance if less [...] M, Birmingham B0 2RJ

[...]nk plc, registered in England under number 1117305, whose registered office is at

[...]ee le.com) and Entranet (www.entranet.co.uk.)

back to **marbles**

get **marbles**™ Safe Shopping Promise

apply now
find out more
details
▸ application status
my account

check your
application status

help

get **marbles**™ online application

▸ apply now
find out more
details
application status
my account

Before you fill out an application form why not make a cup of tea and get your bank and salary details together? We don't want to waste your time by making you apply unnecessarily, so please make sure you can say "Yes" to the following questions:

apply now

get a free CD

■ Is your marbles card for personal use?
■ Do you live in the UK or the Channel Islands?
■ Are you 21 or over?
■ Do you have a household income of more than £5,500 a year?
■ Do you have a good credit record?

If the answers "Yes" to all these questions, click on the 'apply now' button above. This will open up a new window on your PC and will take a few seconds to load.

If you couldn't answer "Yes" to all of the above it is unlikely that you will be accepted. However, if your circumstances do change in the future we would be happy to hear from you.

3

1 2 3
What else for the Marbles credit card site except marbles large and small, each a hyperlink to sub-pages featuring an on-line application form, account details, and so on.

MasterCard
International

•MasterCard
Exclusives Online™
•Our Cards
•Shop Online
•Cardholder
Services
•For Businesses
•Public Sectors/
Organizations
•Sports
Sponsorships
•About Our
Company
•Regional
Websites

Sign
and s
more

Mas

M

Home
Search The Site
View The Site Map
Problems & Questions

Welcome to **Goldfish**

- **GOLDFISH CREDIT CARDS**
- **GOLDFISH GUIDES**

4 5 6 7
The Goldfish site
(5,6,7) opens with a
friendly home page
featuring a pair of
goldfish and a link to
subpages. Goldfish
makes clever use of
credit card shapes to
underline its identity.
A relatively old hand
in the credit card
market, Mastercard
www.mastercard.com
(4) employs a
theatrical, modern
spin on the traditional
scroll bars.

113

4

• ATM Locator • Emergency Services • For Business   **?**

www.mastercard.com

Welcome To MasterCard

Inside you
  will find ...

  ▸ A chance to win a
    new home
  ▸ Celebrity chat
  ▸ Instant gift
  ▸ Gift finder

Choose A Card

APPLY FOR A
CARD

Find the card that's right for you!

Save Time

Stop writing
checks... pay
monthly bills
automatically!

llet

a breeze!

s Online™

6

a Goldfish of your own
Everything you wanted to know about owning and caring for a Goldfish

- Choosing your Goldfish
- Loveable qualities
- Cut the cost of living
- Hidden talents
- The one that got away

Click Here to get the Plug-in for the enhanced animated site

APPLY **NOW**

7

BACK TO INTRO

Loveable qualities

- Everything you'd expect
  from a credit card....
- ....and something you
  might not
- Thinking of switching from
  another card?
- If you're out of action, we'll
  look after your Goldfish

APPLY **NOW**

CHOOSING
YOUR GOLDFISH   LOVEABLE
QUALITIES   CUT THE COST
OF LIVING   HIDDEN
TALENTS   THE ONE THAT
GOT AWAY

RINGING THE CHANGES

Mobile phone company Ericsson **www.ericsson.com** is synonymous with "urban professional" chic. Its site reinforces this with crisp, starchy-white backgrounds flattered by slick black and cool blue. Telecom giant AT&T **www.att.com** opts for pure information.

ERICSSON   Design

Main menu
Design
▶ Accessories
New menu system
Try the phone
Profiles
Voice dialling
Dual band and e-GSM
Vibrating Alert
Active flip
Games
Performance
Consumer package

Open / close flip
Click here to open
and close the flip.

Change angle
Click here to view the
T28 at various angles.

Choose colour
Click here to pick a
colour of your choice.

Mountain Heather

The toughest call is picking the colour
Not much bigger than a credit card, but big on features, this sleek, lightweight phone is fit for any setting. The colours, including Slate Blue, Marble Beige, Urban Grey and rustic Mountain Heather are eye-catching too. Now pick one. If you can.

ERICSSON   Main menu

Main menu
Design
▶ Accessories
New menu system
Try the phone
Profiles
Voice dialling
Dual band and e-GSM
Vibrating Alert
Active flip
Games
Performance
Consumer package

Mobile Phone T28

Combining style with intelligence

The story continues...

Welcome to the enhanced presentation of the T28.
Click here to enter the quick version. (demands no plug-ins)

1 2 3 4

Corporate color schemes set the style at Ericsson's Web site. Subtle, imaginative use of Flash animation ensures an elegance sometimes lacking on competitors' sites— this one's for the grown-ups!

2

ERICSSON

Mobile Phone
T20
Designed to touch
your senses

The T20 was announced by chart-topping R'n'B-group All Saints end of October in London. It is the world's first mobile phone to support SwatchⓇ Internet time. This global concept eliminates time zones making it an ideal format to use when synchronising the time of a live Webcast or letting your friends know when you go online.

The T20 lets you chat with whoever you want, whenever and wherever via SMS or WAP. Attach the FM radio or MP3-player to it and dig your favourite beats. Wear it the way you want to. The Ericsson T20 lets you show who you are.

CLICK ON ONE OF THE PHONE PATTERNS ABOVE
TO ENTER THE WEBSITE!

This site is optimized for IE 4 or better and NS 4 or better

You'll also need to have a Flash 4 plugin and a plugin for Shockwave.
Download Plugin

3

Chatpen™   ERICSSON

SENDING YOUR WORDS FURTHER ✓

To view this site you need Shockwave Flash. If you can't see the animated text you'll need to download the plug-in. Click on the pen to continue.

Download Shockwave Flash
Enter site >>

4

WELCOME TO AT&T

Tues., July 11, 2000

ABOUT AT&T
FOR HOME
FOR BUSINESS
DIRECTORIES
ACCOUNT MANAGEMENT
AS ADVERTISED

Tell Me More!

AT&T connects you with wireless, long distance and local phone, the Internet, cable TV, and beyond...

AT&T Business Internet Services

The internet access with the business attitude.

Search [   ] go

Advanced Search
Site Map
A to Z Index

Enter AT&T Keyword or Search Terms

Stock Info: AT&T 31.88 -1.12   Jul 11, 3:12 pm ET

stay ahead of the game

AT&T
Small Business Center
> > > click

AT&T business network
One Integrated Experience℠

Win a
Trip for 2
to Hawaii
> click for details

Important
News
for AT&T Basic Plan
customers

AT&T
• AT&T B
• AT&T A
  Require
• AT&T W
  Wireles

What's
• Get help
• Small B
• Get the

AT&T DATA & IP SERVICES
Keeping the Promise of the Internet™

IP SERVICES HOME
OVERVIEW
BENEFITS
OPTIONS & PRICING INFORMATION
SERVICE AVAILABILITY & ORDERING
FAQS
TECHNICAL INFORMATION

AT&T DSL Internet Service

AT&T is ready for the new millenium. Move your business into the next century with faster Internet access ... AT&T DSL Internet Service.

What's So Exciting About
AT&T DSL Internet Service?
(Digital Subscriber Line)

DSL
X 28.8

Up to 50 times faster than a 28.8 modem

Its ability to transform your existing, one dimensional phone line into a powerful multidimensional communication system that can take you and your business where you need to go into the next century. With AT&T DSL Internet Service, you can access audio, video, and enhanced graphics over the Internet and through remote LAN access with download speeds that are up to 50 times faster than a 28.8 Kbps modem and 25 times faster than a 56 Kbps modem. DSL technology works over copper wire phone lines simply, easily, and cost-effectively.

AT&T DSL Internet Service

offers high-speed access up to

50 times faster   than a 28.8 modem over existing phone lines

With DSL technology, you won't sit in the waiting-to-receive mode. You'll never hear a busy signal again because there's no need to dial in – the connection is always on. Internet access is included on one low monthly service price.

You'll never hear a busy signal!

AT&T DSL Internet Service offers a range of managed solutions to meet a variety of needs, from the small office/home office (SOHO) to the large corporation that's connecting telecommuters and branch offices.

Welcome to
AT&T Data & IP Services

Order Now and Save – Multi-user Installation Fee Waived Now Through 9/30/00

Click here for our national roll-out schedule for DSL

Get Your Biz a Website

AT&T Business Internet Services

Architecture Overview

LAN

PC   10BaseT   Multi-User
         HUB   DSL Local Loop   Access Network
PC   10BaseT   DSL Router

AT&T IP Backbone

Customer Location

Single User   DSL Local Loop   Access Network

Single User

Your DSL line will simply look like an additional phone line – and your flat-rate monthly charges, determined by the level of service you purchase, will allow unlimited DSL access.

5 6 7 8

AT&T has chosen a white background, but overlays it with a confusing layout that scrolls vertically.

The AT&T Web pages make up for any perceived lack of style with friendly practicality.

TV HEAVEN

The 24-hour news channel CNN **www.cnn.com** is noted for its scattershot approach to current affairs, presenting continually updated news items from around the world. Deutsche Welle **www.dwelle.de** manages its many outlets coolly and calmly. Both stations continue their TV approach in their Web sites: Deutsche Welle confirms its reputation for structure and CNN crams in just about everything.

1 2 3
The Deutsche Welle **www.dwelle.de** site supports its news, radio, TV and online services with cool, clean colors and simplistic—even crude—design.

4

CNN.com

Search
CNN.com [▼]   [Find]

Play video
Watch more CNN VIDEO

myCNN | Video | Audio | Headline News Brief | Free E-mail | Feedback

July 13, 2000 -- Updated 04:17 p.m. EDT, 2017 GMT, @ 868 swatch◻ internet time

MAINPAGE
WORLD
U.S.
WEATHER
BUSINESS
SPORTS
TECHNOLOGY
SPACE
HEALTH
ENTERTAINMENT
POLITICS
LAW
TRAVEL
FOOD
ARTS & STYLE
BOOKS
NATURE
IN-DEPTH
ANALYSIS
LOCAL

myCNN
Headline News brief
news quiz
daily almanac

MULTIMEDIA:
video
video archive
audio
multimedia showcase
more services

FEATURES:
Law Center: The Scopes monkey trial revisited

Does it pay to junk the clunker?

In Other News:
- United States, Vietnam sign historic trade pact | Live : President Clinton announcement on U.S.-Vietnam trade agreement Real or Windows Media ▶
- Arafat, Barak 'grappling with core issues' at Camp David summit ▶
- AIDS is leaving a generation of orphans

5

Korea States of War

HIGHLIGHT
Kwangju at 20
A bloody uprising at Kwangju in 1980 is still a factor in U.S.-South Korea relations

117

latest news ◩
feedback ✉

FEATURES
• Overview
• War Anniversary
• Leader Profiles
• View from the North
• View from the South
• Korean Economy
• Kwangju at 20
• Moscow Connection

...OUT THE WAR
• Interviews
• Profiles
• Documents
• War Map
• War Game

...OUT KOREA
• Timeline
• Maps/At-a-Glance
• Photo Galleries
• Quiz

CNN.com weather

Play video
Watch more CNN VIDEO

myCNN | Video | Audio | Headline News Brief | Free E-mail | Feedback

CNN Sites [▼]
MAINPAGE
WORLD
U.S.
WEATHER
weather maps
storm center
allergy report
biz traveler
world time
BUSINESS
SPORTS
TECHNOLOGY
SPACE
HEALTH
ENTERTAINMENT
POLITICS
LAW
TRAVEL
FOOD
ARTS & STYLE
BOOKS
NATURE
IN-DEPTH
ANALYSIS
LOCAL

myCNN
Headline News brief
news quiz
daily almanac

Extreme weather returns to Europe

Extreme weather conditions have revisited much of Europe this week, with cold and rain descending on the British isles, snow falling on parts of France, and sweltering heat stifling parts of Bulgaria, Turkey and Greece.

FULL STORY

Drought devastating farmers in Southern U.S.

Crouching in a field pockmarked with stunted plants,

FOUR-DAY FORECASTS FOR 8,000 CITIES WORLDWIDE
Enter your U.S. zip code:
[GO]
Zip goes to nearest of 8,000 cities
Or, choose a state:
Select [▼]
Or, browse the text listing:
Complete listing of U.S. states

Choose a World Region:
Select [▼]

Weather Maps:
Check the latest worldwide satellite maps and animated radar maps for U.S. states. View the maps.

Storm Center:
Find out what to do during a hurricane, review storm names and visit storm-related sites. Visit the storm center.

Allergy Report:

Play video
Watch more CNN VIDEO

CNN.com NewsNet
CNN Sites [▼]
Search
CNN.com [▼]
[Find]
CNN.com

TOP STORIES

Bradley endorses Gore's presidential bid

United States, Vietnam sign historic trade pact

Arafat, Barak 'grappling with core issues' at Camp David summit

AIDS is leaving a generation of orphans

(MORE)

BUSINESS
Profits power Nasdaq
Ford takes $3.3B charge in 2Q

4 5 6
As an international channel, CNN has to include a lot of information. The jumbled site lacks the spacious order of that of Deutsche Welle.

BRAND NEW BRANDING

The BBC's Web pages **www.bbc.co.uk** seem comfortably familiar—like worn but favorite shoes. There's sufficient corporate branding to ensure that visitors are aware of where they are, and the Gill type and bold colors set against white backgrounds serve to reinforce the BBC's worldwide broadcasting authority. By contrast, the only style continuity within Discovery's **www.discovery.com** busy pages is the navigation menu.

2

BBC Two's flagship current affairs programme with its award-winning journalism and innovative films from around the world is available every night on the Internet. Click on **Latest Programme** to see the programme live at 21.30 GMT (22.30 BST) each weeknight after which each edition will be available to be viewed again until the next programme. Below you can also see a selection of items from recent programmes. And, as always, Newsnight will be putting the movers and shakers on the spot for the news behind the headlines.

Another chance to see...

What happens when family life collides with political posture?

Underage drinking and subsequent lying to the police. It happens every week. But on Wednesday night one of those who did it was Euan Blair.

The Blairs have claimed to want to keep their family life private, while,

1 2
Simple, strong designs and plenty of familiar faces ensure that the BBC Web site is a home from home, especially for U.K. viewers.

3
Though vertically scrolling, the BBC site offers hyperlinks to sub-pages wherever greater detail is required to tell a story.

Discovery's Web site uses bold colors, big type and enticing images to attract its younger visitors. Each page is subject-driven, and the only common thread from page to page is Discovery's horizontal menu bar. These, too, are cluttered, with a host of navigation options available on each.

119

A GOOD READ

Publications on the Web tend to fall into two design camps: Those which originate in the "real world," such as *Memphis Magazine* www.memphismagazine. com, tend to use their existing designs for their Web page. Exclusively e-publications, like Wine Skinny www.wineskinny.com, sidestep traditional page layouts altogether and make full use of multimedia effects.

2

120

1 2

Memphis Magazine's site (*above*) relies on the printed magazine's prescence, while wine fiends' e-zine www. wineskinny.com (*left*) dispenses with tradition and opts for a design that could work only on the Web.

3

The *USA Today* site (www.usatoday.com) retains the familiar style of its paper version, but may be better known for its front page news items than front end design.

5

The Guardian
The Observer

27.06.2000
Register

filmUnlimited

Unlimited sites | Useful stuff

Home | News | Reviews | Features | Close up | Now showing | On video | Talk | Search | Help

Unlimited
sites,
unlimited
English
**How to use
Guardian
Unlimited in
EFL classes**

4 5 6 7 8

The award-winning
Guardian newspaper
has always had a
design focus, so it's no
surprise to find that
its on-line version is
equally worthy of
merit.

Two-thirds off
tickets for
Beau Travail
and Claire
Denis
interview

**Fowl
language**
Chicken
Run
decoded for
the US

www.★.co.uk

Buy
entertainment
books at bol.com

Make your film vote
count in "The Stel..
film awards

Latest news

Hitchhiker's Guide movie is holding out for
a hero

Affleck tipped to play a younger Jack Ryan

What's on near me..
Enter your postcode:

[ ] [Go]

Film search

[ ] [Go]

6

British Press Awards
Register

GuardianUnlimited
network

Network home | Latest | The Guardian | Our sites | Talk | Jobs | Webguides | Information

Books
Read the
opening of Julie
Myerson's
spooky new tale

Debate
Human genome
experts discuss
the issues

Money
How to stay in
the pink and out
of the red if
you're gay

Tuesday 27 June 2000

Services

Email services and other
platforms
My portfolio
Free content for your site

Search

[Go]
Advanced search
Today's news

Breaking news
Desktop headlines
Today's issues
News quiz
Columnists
Special reports

The Guardian

Front page
All stories
UK news
Politics
International
Business
Comment
Sport

Top stories

Mugabe party wins election
Ruling party narrowly fights off challenge
from Zimbabwe's opposition.
Audio: Jonathan Steele in Harare
Analysis: Mugabe defies critics
Graphic: full results
Cartoon: Steve Bell
Special report

Royals 'should leave palace' – Mowlam
Special report
Comment from Julia Langdon

Interactive

Quiz: How good a complainer are you?

Good
News.
Books at bol.com

Euro 2000
Subscribe here for
your daily update

breathe

Julie Andrews
interviewed
**Watch our
live webcast**

..aily
..teractive
..ossword

click

**career
manager**

Your own page:
finds suitable jobs
for you and stores
ads you like

**education
Unlimited**
Features, talk, web
help and more

**Jobs &
money**
Sort out your life.
Every week.

educationUnlimited
courses schools colleges graduates TEFL universities

HOME AWAY FROM HOME

Ikea's busy site **www.ikea.com** attracts the eye without confusing it. Here, a jumble of shapes and colors comes together in a satisfying smorgasbord. The utterly contemporary home page is immediately appealing, engaging the casual visitor and committed buyer alike.

1
Ikea's home page looks for all the world like the cover of a catalogue—dare to put it down!

2
Who could resist a virtual visit to the Ikea-styled homes of real people from around the globe? Peek, and be inspired.

select a country » [IKEA around the World ⬍]

select a country: [IKEA around the World ▼]

better living

Visit homes around the world and discover what smart solutions people used to help create better everyday living situations.

living with kids

Discover all of the fun stuff, as well as practical kids furnishings, that IKEA has for the most important people in the world!

product guide

You'll find some of our most popular products along with assembly tips, interactive guides and inspirational ideas.

about IKEA

What's in a name? Find out about IKEA, our unique design approach and how we keep prices so low and quality so high!

IKEA near you

Everything you need to know about visiting IKEA. And our Store Directory can help locate the IKEA store near you.

spring forward

what's new

Bring the freshness of spring into your home and garden with ideas from IKEA. Click here for products that help you greet the season.

• • • • • • • •

Illuminate every room in your home with just the right lights. Get inspirational ideas and lighting advice with the IKEA Guide to Brighter Living.

• • • • • • • •

International competitions recognise IKEA for product innovation and ecologically friendly designs. Find out which IKEA products took home awards.

• • • • • • • •

An IKEA classic, POÄNG is a comfortable, functional chair that has an incredible number of options. The "your POÄNG" design tool allows you to find the right cushion, colour and frame for your style.

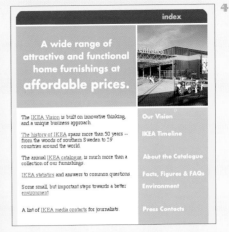

index

A wide range of attractive and functional home furnishings at affordable prices.

The IKEA Vision is built on innovative thinking, and a unique business approach.

Our Vision

The history of IKEA spans more than 50 years -- from the woods of southern Sweden to 29 countries around the world.

IKEA Timeline

The annual IKEA catalogue, is much more than a collection of our furnishings.

About the Catalogue

IKEA statistics and answers to common questions.

Facts, Figures & FAQs

Some small, but important steps towards a better environment!

Environment

A list of IKEA media contacts for journalists.

Press Contacts

3 4
Here, the Web pages seem to reflect the ethos of Ikea: allusions to modernity while safely contemporary.

5 6
Despite the uncool pop-up menu with HTML type, Ikea's layouts bring colorful, affordable chic to a post-modern world.

123

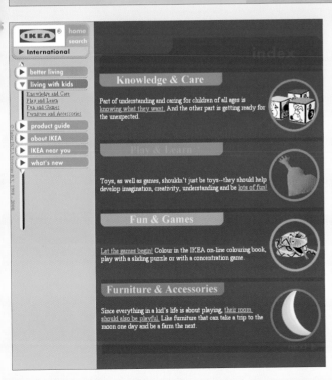

HIGH FLYERS

Useless clutter is the last thing you want when booking a flight on the Web. Air France **www.airfrance.com** and Delta Vacations **www.deltavacations.com** both present vast amounts of information in a workable way that remains attractive and practical. The Air France site is authoritative and convincing, while Delta opts for a more informal look.

1

Browse Packages

Paris Packages

France & Monaco Packages

Europe Packages

Concorde Vacations

AIR FRANCE
holidays

Special Offers

1 2 3
The Air France site is easy to use and welcoming.

Cater to your soul.
$1,089.*

Monaco

Monte-Carlo from $1,089.

Let your heart take off and soar into the depths of the imagination and the magic of the Monaco with Air France Ho to Nice from New York (JFK or Newark), 5 night first class (FC), superior first class (SFC), or deluxe (DLX) accomoda daily.

To further enhance your stay, enjoy a six-day car rental for $79**

Hotels	Class	April 1 — June 15 Sept 1 — Oct 31	June 16 — Aug 31
Abela Hotel Monaco	FC	$1089	$1369
Hotel Mirabeau	SFC	$1269	$1515
Le Meridien Beach Plaza	SFC	$1285	$1879
Hotel Hermitage	DLX	$1345	$1589

homepage   packages   terms and conditions   e-mail us

MO

for more
the m
www.mon

AIR FRANCE
holidays

French Riviera

golden days, glittering nights
[prices from $969]

Life's a beach! Coast down to La Croisette, the casinos and more for a glamorous glimpse of the good life.

● 5 nights/6 days
● Round-trip air to Nice on Air France
● 5 nights hotel accommodation in Nice, Cannes, Juan Les Pins or Monte Carlo including service charges and VAT
● Continental or buffet breakfast daily
● Stop-over in Paris permitted at no extra charge

Package price per person, twin or double occupancy for 5 nights including round-trip air from New York or Newark with midweek departures April 1 - Oct 31, 2000.

Select Box	Hotel Name	Break-fast	April 1 — June 15 Sept 1 — Oct 31	Extra night	June 16 — Aug 31	Extra night
Nice						
○	Mercure Nice Centre Notre Dame	🍴	$969	$66	$1235	$69
○	Mercure Promenade Des Anglais	🍴	$985	$69	$1229	$69

homepage   packages   terms and   e-mail us
conditions   **Step 1: Please select a hotel**   proceed to
next step ➤

3

4

▲.Delta Vacations™

Select your vacation destination and experience the world through Delta Vacations.

Delta Vacations

Home

Internet Deals

Promotions

Destinations

Bahamas & Caribbean
Bermuda
Cancun & Mexico
Europe
Eastern Europe & The World
Florida/Beaches
Golf
Hawaii
Las Vegas
Latin America
Orlando
Ski
U.S.A. & Canada
Walt Disney World® Resort

Sign Up

Groups

Travel Agents

Corporate Program

Your Reservation

USA & Canada ○

Las Vegas ○

Ski ○

Florida ○

Walt Disney World® Resort ○

Hawaii ○

○ Bahamas & Caribbean

○ Bermuda

○ Mexico

○ Latin America

○ Europe

○ Eastern Europe & The World

4 5
Delta Vacations' easy-to-navigate site provides the essential travel information—including weather updates—with a lively, swinging style.

5

▲.Delta Vacations™

Caribbean & Bahamas

Delta Vacations

Home

Internet Deals

Promotions

Destinations

Bahamas & Caribbean
Bermuda
Cancun & Mexico
Europe
Eastern Europe & The World
Florida/Beaches
Golf
Hawaii
Las Vegas
Latin America
Orlando
Ski
U.S.A. & Canada
Walt Disney World® Resort

Sign Up

Groups

Travel Agents

Corporate Program

One of the most desirable vacation destinations in the world, the Caribbean and the Bahamas boasts an impressive array of distinctions. Pristine beaches, tropical breezes, unsurpassed natural beauty, fine shopping and various watersports. Soothe your soul and prepare to delve into an unforgettable island experience.

Featured Vacation

The Westin Rio Mar Beach Resort & Casino
San Juan
click here for information

Where do you want to take your vacation? Choose below.

- Aruba
- Bermuda
- Grand Cayman
- Nassau & Paradise Island
- Jamaica
- Puerto Rico
- U.S. Virgin Islands
- St. Lucia
- Turks and Caicos

A FINE EXHIBIT

Nederlands   English   Deutsch   Français   Italiano

W hen it comes to making visually interesting
arrangements, museums are ideally placed—
translating those arrangements to the Web, however, is
another matter entirely. Two of the better sites are the
Rijksmuseum's at **www.rijksmuseum.nl** and the Design
Museum's at **www.designmuseum.org**. Subtle layouts
and items from the museums' exhibits combine with
cool colors to give a deserved air of authority.

1 2 3
www.rijksmuseum.nl
uses dramatic,
enlarged details of its
exhibits as underlying
imagery for the Flash-
based interface. The
fluidity of the design
creates a captivating
snapshot of its
collection, subtly
enticing the e-tourists
through its turnstiles.

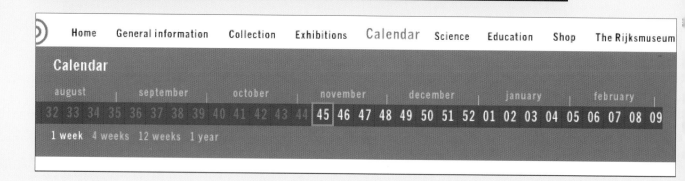

Design museum
South Bank by Tower Bridge

Discovery

Design museum
South Bank by Tower Bridge

Discovery   Exhibitions   Education   Shop/Cafe   Supporting the Museum   Information   Special Events

6

Design museum
South Bank by Tower Bridge

Enter **Flash** Version (Full Content)   Enter **HTML** Version (Reduced Content)

design sense

For information about **Design Sense 2000**
see the **Call for Entries**

4 5 6 7 8
There's that white background again! Gorgeous, saturated colors leap from the screen when set against a crisp, white backdrop. This combination is the choice for so many high-quality sites, including that of London's Design Museum.

Philips Toaster 1996
Designer: Philips Corporate Design
with Allessandro Mendini/Alessi

The shop of contemporary design and riverside cafè enable visitors to indulge and relax. Situated on the ground floor visitors can enjoy both the cafè and shop with or without a visit to the galleries.

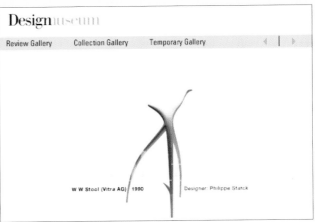

Design museum

Review Gallery   Collection Gallery   Temporary Gallery

W W Stool (Vitra AG) 1990   Designer: Philippe Starck

THE COLOR OF SOUND

Record companies have a particularly acute awareness that presentation, through strong design, sells. Leading consumer electronics company Sony **www.sony.com** has plumped for a high-tech, dynamic feel for its home page, backed by hand drawn sub-pages (which, frankly, fail to work). Whereas Motown **www. motown.com** oozes laid-back style.

2

1 2
The Sony site's confused layout and turgid colors are not especially welcoming.

3 4
The choice of contrasts lacks coherence. Click past the home page and you're presented with these unattractive hand-drawn image maps and keylines, which look like they were thrown together with a cheap paint package.

3

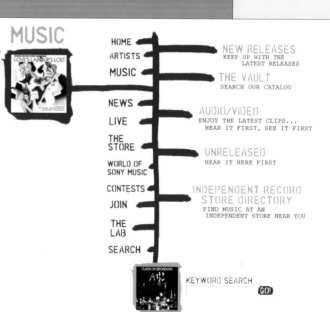

5 6 7 8

Not surprisingly, cool blues and groovy grays feature heavily on the Classic Motown site. Fun design and clever use of Flash abound, but, more importantly, **www.motown.com** brings a new, different dimension to music presentation by hanging its entire site on a time line, putting its music in context.

COLOR CLASSIC

B enetton's Web page **www.benetton.com** is the classic example of good design in print translating to good design on the Web. Strong typography, bold colors on white backgrounds, and repeats of the clothing company's well-known advertising campaigns make the site visually interesting yet instantly familiar.

I

UNITED COLORS OF BENETTON

WHO WE ARE   WHAT WE SAY   WHAT WE MAKE

Fabrica Cinema Productions wins
Special Jury Prize
at the Cannes Film Festival

BLACKBOARDS
a film by Samira Makhmalbaf

COLORS
OBJECTS
Colors Extra/Ordinary
Objects Exhibition in Florence,
June 22nd - July 16th

MUSEUM LELEQUE
The Museum of Patagonia
opens its doors

INVESTOR RELATIONS   CONTACT   WHAT DO YOU NEED?

copyright Benetton 1999/2000

2

ALL HUMAN BEING[S]

FREE AND [   ]

IN DIGNITY

WHAT

ABOUT WHO WE ARE
Our Businesses
Our Communications

ABOUT W[   ]
Fabrica
Colors
Playlife
Catalogs

COL

a magazine about the rest of t[   ]

I 2
Underlined hyperlinks aside, Benetton's home page is a straightforward lesson in textbook graphic design.

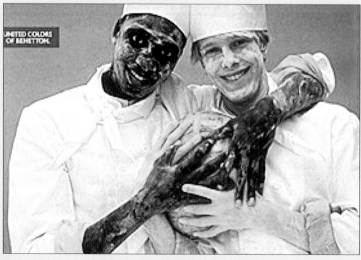

5

6

3

131

VE SAY

ABOUT WHO YOU ARE
People and Places
United Colors Divided Opinions

ORS

www.colorsmagazine.com

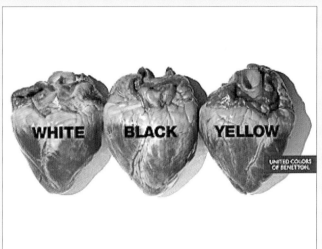

4

7

3 4
It's possible to use fun images in a way that would almost certainly offend were they presented to a non-Net audience.

5 6 7
The company's powerful billboard campaigns work as well on the Web as they do on the street.

INSIDE KNOWLEDGE

Intel's processors power most computers that access the Web—and lots of those which provide it. The company has sidestepped loads of special effects and opted instead for a cool and essentially elegant Web site **www.intel.com**. Though it has a "traditional" framed Web layout, the site works well and has a friendly feel.

1 2

Intel's cool blue home page is reminiscent of a corporate brochure or in-house magazine. Buttons, a header bar, and strong central images are used to good effect.

3 4 5

Subpages are packed with added-value offerings, such as desktop wallpaper, screensavers, a virtual computer clinic, and tips pages.

1

- Intel.com
- Contents
- Search

Select a Country

- Home Computing
- Business
- Developer
- Channel

- Products/Services
- Company Info

Making

2

- Intel.com
- Contents
- Search
- Contact Us
- Support

intel

Select a Country

- Home Computing
- Business
- Developer
- Channel

- Products/Services
- Company Info

- For Pentium® III Processor Owners

Making the Internet
as Powerful as Our Processors

▶ Expanding on its network of world-class Internet Data Centers with the newest opening in Japan, Intel® Online Services provides reliable, mission-critical solutions for the Internet economy.

▶ Prioritize Network Traffic
New products deliver faster and better e-Commerce experiences.

▶ Pentium® 4 Processor
Intel announces the brand name of its new microprocessor.

▶ New Internet Hosting Services
Get reliable e-Business solutions with managed hosting options.

*Legal Information and Privacy Policy © 2000 Intel Corporation

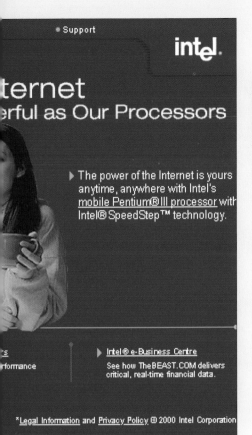

● Support

intel.

ternet
erful as Our Processors

▶ The power of the Internet is yours anytime, anywhere with Intel's mobile Pentium® III processor with Intel® SpeedStep™ technology.

's
rformance

▶ Intel® e-Business Centre
See how TheBEAST.COM delivers critical, real-time financial data.

*Legal Information and Privacy Policy © 2000 Intel Corporation

● Intel.com home   ● product info   ● search   ● contact us   ● support   intel.

● home computing
● Intel® processors for home PCs
● get home product info
● have fun with your PC
● shop with Intel

Subscribe to Home Computing for site updates, product info and more.

Name

E-mail Address

? ● Submit Subscription

Select a
Select a Country ◆

Home Computing
Products, PCs and Ideas for the Home

Read This Month's Feature Article

Traveling with ● Technology

Enhance your vacation with the Internet.

Have Fun With Your PC
Grab software, screensavers, guides and advice for your PC.

Get Home Products Info
Select from a range of Intel® home computing products.

Pentium® III Processor
Experience the best of the Web with the Pentium® III processor and Intel® WebOutfitter℠ service.

Updates

Intel PC Buyer's Guide
Find the PC that's just right for you with the Intel PC Buyer's Guide. Just answer a few questions, and we'll recommend a system configuration and peripherals based on your answers.

Increase performance with the new family of Intel® Pentium® III processors.
Intel® Pentium® III processors are available for your home or small office PC at speeds up to 1.0GHz. You can also get power on the move with mobile Pentium III processors for your laptop PC, available at speeds up to 750MHz and featuring Intel® SpeedStep™ technology.

Intel® AnyPoint™ Wireless Home Network
Share simultaneous Internet access, files, drives, printers and more—without wires. Introducing Intel® AnyPoint™ Wireless Home Network products for laptop and desktop PCs.

◄ back to top

133

● Intel® processors for home PCs
● get home product info
● home computing
● Intel® processors for home PCs
● get home product info
● have fun with your PC

● Download Software and Games
● Screensavers and Wallpaper
● Discover Useful Tips and Tricks
● Learn PC Basics
● Calculate Download Times

● shop with Intel

Subscribe to Home Computing for site updates, product info and more.

Name

E-mail Address

? ● Submit Subscription

● product info   ● search   ● contact us   ● support   intel.

Have Fun
with Your PC

Download Software and Games   more ▶
Check out games and software demos optimized for the Intel® Pentium® III processor.

Screensavers and Wallpaper   more ▶
Dress up your monitor with fun screensavers and wallpaper designed for your PC.

Discover Useful Tips and Tricks   more ▶
Discover great ways to get more from your PC and keep it running at peak performance.

Learn PC Basics   more ▶
Get the information you need to understand how PC technology can work for you.

Calculate Download Times   more ▶

Maximize your Internet usage by calculating and planning download times.

what's new

Alex Builds His Farm¹
Download fun wallpaper and screensavers to bring the farm to your PC.

Laura's Happy Adventures²
Get fun and decorative goodies for your PC.

◄ back to top

● Intel.com home   ● product info   ● search   ● contact us   ● support   intel.

● home computing
● products & services
● shopping

fun stuff
● Alex's Home Page
● Screensaver
● Wallpaper

buy it now at
Shop Intel ▶

Home Computing
Fun Stuff

Alex Builds His Farm²

Screensaver
Bring the fun from Alex and the original PLAYMOBIL® farm to your PC with this colorful screensaver.

Wallpaper
Enjoy the look of the country with colorful scenes from Alex's farm on your desktop.

◄ back to top

*Legal Information and Privacy Policy © 2000 Intel Corporation

KISS AND MAKE UP

Cosmetics giant Revlon **www.revlon.com** combines sassy visuals with layouts straight from the magazine pages for a Web site that looks exactly "right." The company has avoided the use of exclusively Web-oriented entities almost completely—apart from a hyperlink or two—and the result is perfectly matched to its target audience. The Lipstick Librarian at **www.teleport.com/~petlin/liplib** is a tongue-in-cheek on-line agony aunt that uses a layout reminiscent of all things rock 'n' roll.

134

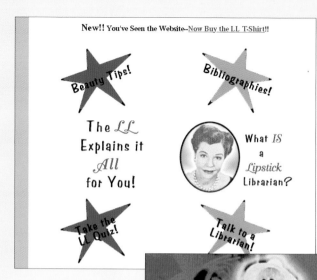

New!! You've Seen the Website--Now Buy the LL T-Shirt!!

Beauty Tips!

Bibliographies!

The *LL* Explains it *All* for You!

What *IS* a *Lipstick Librarian*?

Take the LL Quiz!

Talk to a Librarian!

2

She's *Bold!!*

She's *Sassy!!*

She's *Helpful!!*

She's ...

"Don't filter out **this** site! - Karen Schneider

"Fresh, fun and funky—just like my **last** showing!" —Issac Mizrahi

"You're <u>still</u> here?!?!" —*American Libraries*

The Lipstick Librarian!

5

1 2

The Lipstick Librarian's Web site sports a design that a 1950s *Practical Householder* magazine would be proud of. An eclectic layout breaks modern rules but presents a funky retro-styled design that has full-on pulling power!

4

3

new feature:

HOW TO BUY
online | retail

REVLON

SUMMER 2000

Bamboo
BLAST

Color blasts off! Skin glows.

REVLON
R E P O R T

COSMETICS
revlon makeup

FRAGRANCE
fresh sense

HAIR
color & care

BEAUTY TOOLS
tools & tips

TRAVEL RETAIL
duty free

FLIP & MIX
try a new look

GIVEAWAYS
talk to us

CORPORATE
business info

135

3 4 5 6

Gorgeous colors backed with slick visuals ensure that Revlon's Web site is bang on target. Revlon is among the few who have transcended the Web's design boundaries to create a layout that would work in any situation.

AquaBlast

A blast of blue on sunkissed skin—It's color as accessory: Match it up or mix it up.

Tips&Toes

Add shock waves to tips and toes with AquaBlast. GLAM TIP: Add a golden touch to feet with Face & Body Gleamer in Gilded.

Eyes, Lips
and Face

Click to see.

Back to
summer shades

BambooBlast   SunBlast

Sunstruck neutrals show off all the Bamboo Blast brights.

A blast of solar energy plays against sun-shined skin.

Back...

Super Lustrous Lipstick - Iced Mocha | Revlon Nail Enamel - Bamboo
Face & Body Gleamer - Gilded

Lips - Iced Mocha | Eyes & Nails - SunBlast | Face & Body Gleamer - Glide

6

BANKING ON IT

anks are among the few sites that are not specifically trying to attract Web visitors. The majority of users are likely to be existing customers checking details of their accounts or potential customers looking to switch from another bank. This rationale equates to sites that do not need to sell themselves primarily as banks, but instead need visual assistance to present their complex service range beyond basic e-banking.

1 2

NatWest (1) is one of the few U.K. banks that has not had to merge in recent times. Strong branding is integral to its on-line strategy. The Union Bank of California (2) presents the user with easy-to-use instructions and very clear explanations.

136

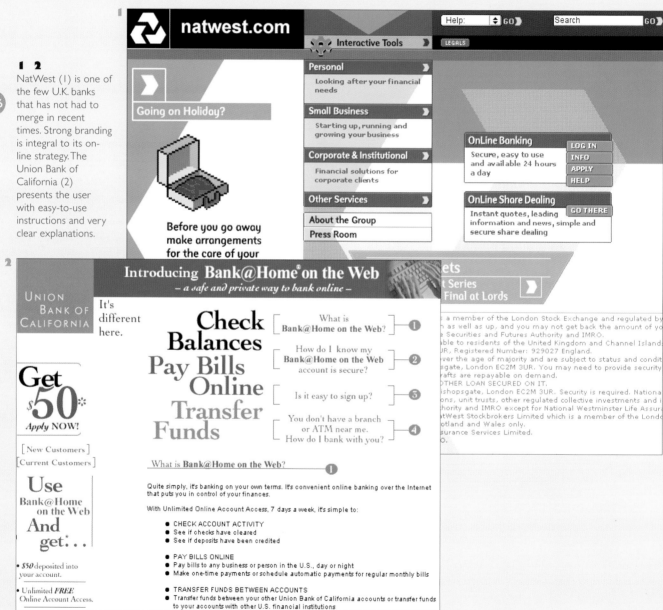

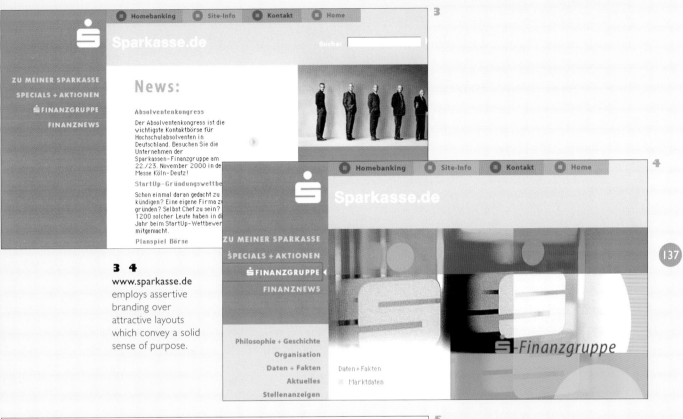

3 4
www.sparkasse.de
employs assertive
branding over
attractive layouts
which convey a solid
sense of purpose.

5 6
The Swiss bank UBS
offers a multitude of
services. Suave,
restrained, and
multilingual, **www.ubs.
com** presents this
complex service
range in an easily
accessible format.

SIMPLE SERMON

These sites show that simple, fun visuals work just as well as the full-on multimedia showcase. Ben & Jerry's **www.benandjerrys.com** has stirred funky images and colorful type into a tasty mixture. Coffee brand Nescafé's opening pages **www.nescafe.com** combine full-blown animated versions of its TV-ad campaigns, with digitized jingles for a captivating multimedia treat.

......Neuerscheinungen

......DetektivStories

......SpielGeschichten

......Alle Titel im Shop

......SpielSpaß

......Tivola Wissen

Site Index | Flavors | Scoop Shops | Gifts | Good Jobs | Fun Stuff | Consumer Assistance | Company Info.

Happy Halloween

Yo, BOO! Here's a shortcut to the best Halloween stuff ever.

Yo, it's Monday, November 13, 2000. Good Evening!

All Natural
BEN & JERRY'S
VERMONT'S FINEST™

Introducing...
Festivus™

Slick Shockwave animations and rich digital sound and jingles make for a rollercoaster ride of multimedia effects at the Nescafé site. Downloads and interesting insights into the coffee-making process add value.

5

139

about Nescafé **coffee people** *coffee world* **downloads** **mailbox** **faqs**

home site map links help

origins tree to cup tips nutrition & health did you know ?   Go Global.. ▲▼

NESCAFÉ.
Nescafé.com

nutrition & health

1 2 3
Ultra-simple cartoon images, alongside funky logos and just enough text to get the message across, create an eye-catching ensemble at both the Tivola **www.tivola.de** (1,2) and Ben & Jerry's (3) sites.

Coffee World

Nutrition & health

Caffeine, the mild stimulant found in coffee, improves alertness and concentration and appears to boost the body's metabolism, improving both mental and physical performance.

Most health professionals consider four cups of coffee a day to be a moderate amount, but experts confirm that 500 - 600mg of caffeine per day (6 cups of fairly strong coffee) is quite safe for most people from a general health point of view. Naturally, this will vary from person to person and depend on what sort of coffee you drink. So here is a quick guide to the caffeine content of different types of coffee, per 150ml:

Ground coffee	80 - 90mg
Instant coffee	60mg
Decaffeinated coffee	3mg

NESCAFÉ.
open up

6

7

A DOG'S LIFE

There's a famous *New Yorker* cartoon that shows a dog sitting at a computer screen, one paw guiding the mouse. Turning to another pooch sitting close by, the dog says, "On the Web, no one knows you're a dog." (A similar joke substitutes "Macintosh user" for dog.) In fact, the only "dogs" you will see are the thousands of desperately awful sites thrown together by the many who offer themselves as Web designers, or those devoted to the genuine (and not so genuine) four-legged article, as shown here.

1 2 3
The Artful Dog site www.artfuldog.com mixes quirky images with a neat logo, practical use of JavaScripts for on-line shopping, and lots of dogs, for a site that is certain to attract dog lovers. All of this proves that clever use of materials can transcend subject matter.

140

"Teammates"

"The Howler"

what's
NEW

Make this your first stop each time you visit us and you'll be kept up to date on all of our latest additions and acquisitions. We're constantly adding new artists and new work, and this is where you'll find it first!

featured
ARTIST

Judy Johnson

We celebrate the Iditarod this month by featuring musher/artist Judy Johnson's images of sled dogs and the great race itself.

BiznessOnline.com
NEW MEDIA DIV.

2

3

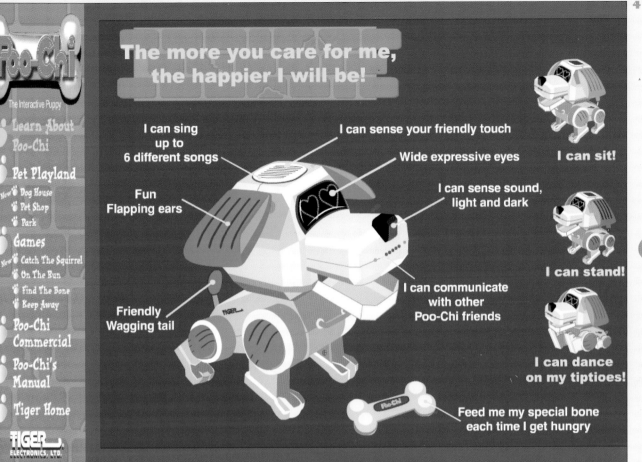

Poo-Chi
The Interactive Puppy

- Learn About Poo-Chi
- Pet Playland
  - *New!* Dog House
  - Pet Shop
  - Park
- Games
  - *New!* Catch The Squirrel
  - On The Run
  - Find The Bone
  - Keep Away
- Poo-Chi Commercial
- Poo-Chi's Manual
- Tiger Home

TIGER
ELECTRONICS, LTD.

The more you care for me, the happier I will be!

I can sing up to 6 different songs

Fun Flapping ears

Friendly Wagging tail

I can sense your friendly touch

Wide expressive eyes

I can sense sound, light and dark

I can communicate with other Poo-Chi friends

Feed me my special bone each time I get hungry

I can sit!

I can stand!

I can dance on my tiptioes!

4 5 6
An industrial-strength color scheme ensures Tiger Toys' Poo-Chi site **www. tigertoys.com/poochi** will appeal to kids of all ages.

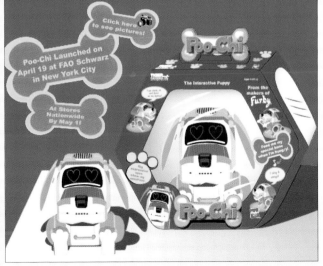

5

6

ALL ACTION

Web sites devoted to kids should be big, bright, and brash, but they don't have to have bad designs. Both the Action Man **www.actionman.com** and Super Soaker **www.supersoaker.com** sites use sophisticated layouts with strong images and plenty of added-value downloads to good effect.

1 2 3
On-line mission instructions, desktop wallpaper downloads, and even a button for parents to click—it's all at the Action Man Web site.

142

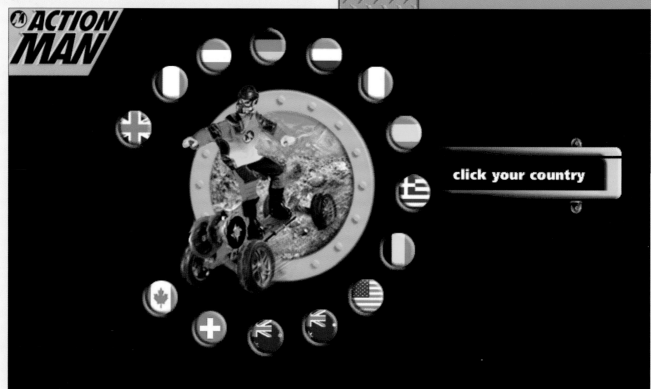

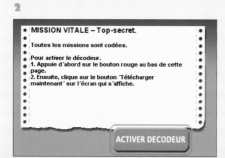

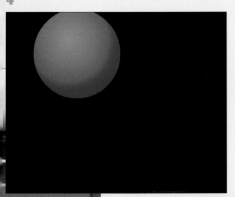

4 | **5** | **4**

4 5 6 7 8 9
Animated splashes
and a water pistol
that moves into view
like an interstellar
craft from *2001: A
Space Odyssey*—that's
Super Soaker's site.

Accès
Autorisé

6

143

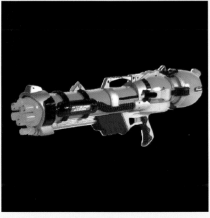

7 | **8** | **9**

THE BIG SHOP

When it comes to selling, "real" supermarkets have honed their presentation skills to a fine degree, employing strategies that assault the senses to ensure that customers make impulse purchases as well as buy the weekly basics. Not surprising, then, that supermarkets know how to present their Web sites to best effect, too. Industry experts predict that home shopping may represent up to 15 to 20 percent of grocery volume by the year 2005.

3

145

Sainsbury's
tasteforlife

www.**sainsburystoyou**.co.uk

home   recipes   wine   organics   Sainsbury's   help desk

organics home | eat organic | all about organics | over to you | organic cafe | 10 reasons | the interview

organicvillage

Welcome to organic village. From delicious recipes to the latest issues and celebrity interviews, whether you're a fully fledged organic consumer or just thinking about switching a few items on your shopping list, here is your complete online guide to all things organic.

The story this week...

An organic farmer is protecting his strawberry crop from an invasion of slugs with the help of an army of hedgehogs

find out more...

eat organic

all about organics

over to you

the interview

organic cafe

10 great reasons to go organic

Food for thought... The Ministry of Agriculture, Fisheries and Food currently spends twice as much testing for pesticides as it does on research and development into organic farming

Log In

, 2000 ShopLink.com, Inc.
600 pixels or higher.
portunities

TESCO

home   shopping   news & features   talking Tesco   help

Home
quick links

groceries online
books
CDs & minidiscs
videos & DVDs
babies & toddlers
home & living

Clubcard
What's in store
Tesco Personal Finance
Quick Tour of Tesco.com

welcome to
Tesco

Shopping online at Tesco.com is quick, easy and great value. As well as delivering your weekly groceries, we now offer books, videos, CDs and a whole lot more. And don't forget you earn Clubcard points too! With Tesco.com shopping just got easier!.

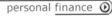

groceries at home ⊙
We can do your shopping for you and deliver it when you want.

personal finance ⊙
From Visa cards to great value mortgages Tesco Personal Finance has the answer

instore ⊙
Find out what's going on in Tesco.

baby & toddler ⊙
We've over 600 products for your baby, toddler or pre-school youngster.

books ⊙
Harry's here at 40% off list price! And we've over a million more titles at great Tesco value.

music & video ⊙
CDs, minidiscs, DVDs or videos. Take your pick!

4

---

1 | 2 | 3 | 4

www.peapod.com, www.shoplink.com, www.sainsbury.co.uk, and www.tesco.com offer up crisp, clean white backgrounds filled with happy, healthy faces and scrumptious foodstuffs, as well as related "impulse buy" products and services. Ally that with entirely practical, frame-based layouts, and you have the recipe for perfect supermarket Web sites—just add e-customers!

GOOD BUY

Commercial enterprise was heavily frowned upon when the Web first threw its doors wide open to a non-academic audience. There are many documented instances of tedious "flame wars" started by the self-appointed guardians of the Net following explicit advertising. Now, thankfully, all that has passed.

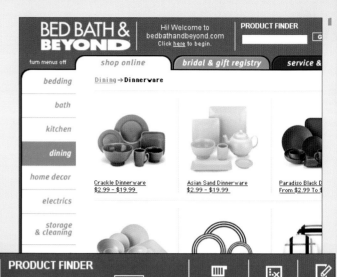

1 2 3
www.bedbathand
beyond.com (1,2)
supports a
straightforward
extension of the
company's printed
catalog with a lifestyle
magazine. Children's
clothing giant
OshKosh B'gosh's site
**www3.oshkoshbgosh.
com** offers lots of
crisp, clean images.

4

BARNES&NOBLE.com
www.bn.com

cart   account   help   order status

Home | Bookstore | eBooks | College Textbooks | Out of Print | Music | DVD& Video | Software | **Prints& Posters** | Magazine Subscriptions | Online Courses

Browse Categories | Browse Collections | Quality&Display

QUICK SEARCH [_____]   SEARCH

Your Shopping Cart
No items in cart.
🛒 Proceed to Checkout

Browse Categories
- Health & Medicine
- Humor
- Magazine Covers
- Maps
- Military
- Nature
- Performing Arts
- Photography
- Propaganda
- Publishing & Mass Media
- Science & Technology
- Sports

more categories...

Great Poster Display Ideas

- See examples of posters and prints in your home or office.
- See the different sizes available on paper or canvas.

▶ Browse Categories
▶ Browse Collections

Prints & Posters gallery

Available on both canvas and PAPER

Harry Potter Canvas Prints
Available only at Barnes & Noble

They loved the books, they can't wait for the movie, and now they can show their Hogwarts pride with an exclusive Harry Potter canvas print. See our display of Harry Potter Canvas Prints.

Harry Potter, characters, names and related indicia are Trademarks of Warner Bros. Copyright 2001.

- Our premium-quality canvases are ready to hang — no framing necessary. Learn more about our product and display ideas.

- Explore our collection of rarely reproduced images, from vintage magazine and book covers to classic and contemporary images.

- Whatever you choose, we will print and ship — on demand — just for you.

Harry Potter Canvas Prints

Featured Collections

Book Jackets
Great book jackets are a joy and an art form unto themselves: one artist's visual interpretation of another artist's words. The

Election Year Images
Politics may make strange bedfellows, but political posters can make fine roommates — decorative ones, that is. Enjoy

147

5

BARNES&NOBLE.com
www.bn.com

cart   account   help   order status

Home | Bookstore | eBooks | College Textbooks | Out of Print | Music | DVD& Video | Software | Prints& Posters | Magazine Subscriptions | Online Courses

Safe Shopping Guarantee | Privacy Policy | Gifts | Kids | eCards | Store Finder

QUICK SEARCH [Books ▾] [_____] SEARCH

Your Shopping Cart
No items in cart.
🛒 Proceed to Checkout

November 13, 2000

VOTE
NEW Classics
SWEEPSTAKES
SPONSORED BY TNT

New at B&N.com
- Free Internet Service
- Easy Returns
- New Classics Sweepstakes

What's This?

Online shopping just got easier! Now Your Shopping Cart is always visible, with a list of items you've selected -- and you can add items without leaving the page you're browsing. When you're done shopping, click Proceed to Checkout, and you're on your way!

▶ More information

Rare, Secondhand & Out of Print

Utterly Original Gifts for True Bibliophiles
Looking for a really unique and elegant gift this year? We've pulled together thousands of gems in our Rare, Secondhand & Out of Print Store, from incunabula and illuminated manuscripts to collectible first editions and secondhand classics. Browse our themed collections for ideas, or search our comprehensive database for a specific title!

▶ Celebrate more than 1,600 years of philosophy and theology in our St. Augustine collection

DESPERATE ALTERNATIVE

Alternative clothes manufacturer Diesel **www.diesel.com** tries ever harder to mix the irony of post-modernism with quirky imagery and off-the-wall tag lines to imbue its product ranges with that indefinable "something." The design has little to do with clothes, but, importantly, it looks right, proving perhaps that the motivational force for on-line layout really isn't so very different.

3

1

2

4

5

VIRTUAL STORES
    United Kingdom

COLLECTIONS
    Spring/Summer 2000
    Diesel
    Kids
    DieselStyleLab
    Denim
    Fragrances
    Spare Parts
    Shades
    Footwear

ADVERTISING
    Successful Living Guides

DIESEL CLUB
    Join Diesel Club

COMMUNICATION
    Email Diesel
    Global Store Listing

DIESEL®
FOR SUCCESSFUL LIVING

ME & MY... ▪ ◪ ▪

149

FELLOW

DIESEL®
FRAGRANCES

WWW.DIESEL.COM

PLUS PLUS

ZERO PLUS
NEW

1 | 2 | 3 | 4 | 5 | 6
The Diesel site is in almost constant flux (like so many other sites on the Web), and the clothing company is always exploring possibilities for quirky imagery to help sell its products to... well, people who would otherwise buy Levi's.

6

SHOUTING FROM THE ROOFTOPS

Few are the sites that manage to sidestep banner advertising, and yet the banner has become almost an art form in itself. Unlike TV and radio advertising, banner ads are almost subliminal—certainly, it's easy to click on past them without even noticing they are there on the page. Bad for the advertisers? Not exactly. The subliminal message is advertising at its most potent. Here follows a selection of some of the better examples.

Two unique design constraints are placed on banner ads: the layout of a banner must fit within another, possibly quite different layout, and the banner itself is supremely limited space-wise.

150

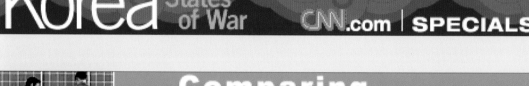

Feeling deflated?

For safe online shopping, health and beauty tips, features and advice.

GAP it's T (and tank) time
essential summer tops now **at gap.com**

Buy the latest album from Enrique at TWEC.COM!

New... On the Web   **Thurs**

 **Give all your letters the personal touch, quickly and easily.**   **With our new and improved Letter Management Tool.**

trade magazines piled high?

save yourself from the info glut

cnnfn.com's IndustryWatch

Fortunately for the designer, banner ads are not static. Almost invariably, banners are continually updated with further information and invitations to click on to the advertiser's site. The animation is cyclic, so the designer has more space to play with—it's just that it's provided in little slices!

HOME FRONT

Innovation in the home has brought the names of what might otherwise be near-invisible companies, such as vacuum-cleaner manufacturer Dyson and product designer Alessi, to the mouths of the masses. But fame has its price: in the new millennium, home-product companies can't be content with being dowdy and beige, as they were in times past. Both Dyson **www.dyson.co.uk** and Alessi **www.alessi.com** have designed Web sites worthy of their new-found status.

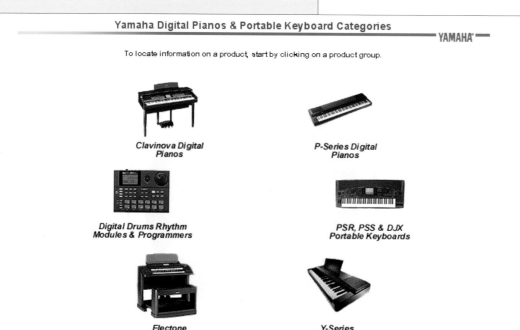

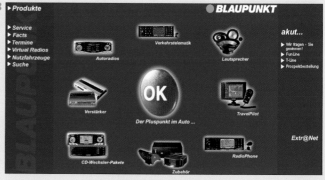

1 | 2 | 3 | 4

Dyson flaunts its curves (1) in a way that is rare in the angular world of the Web. Its sweeping lines, Web-beating buttons and icons clean up. Yamaha (2) keeps it low-key with basic product listings. The Blaupunkt (3,4) site (*below*) proves that a name ("blue dot") and a trademark can be identical.

5

La storia
The history

gli anni /*the years 20/30*
gli anni /*the years 50/70*
gli anni /*the years 80/90*

Designers & Products
Novità primavera '**00**
New products
Progetti speciali
Special projects
La storia/ *The history*
Libreria/*Bookshop*
Worldwide Network
News
On-line Design Competition

Alessi è socio fin dalla fondazione della
"Associazione Imprese Italiane Alta Gamma"

Credits

ALESSI

6

5 6 7
Alessi's Web site is a
fabulous showcase of
products past and
present, but layouts
are on the whole
pedestrian; it's the
products which carry
the site.

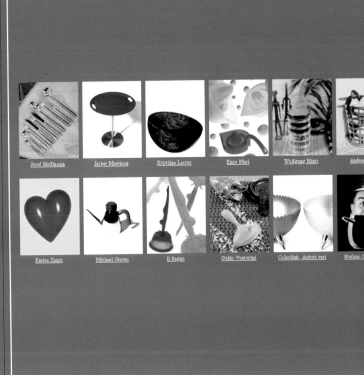

· **Nuovi prodotti** '00
New products

Josef Hoffmann — Jasper Morrison — Kristiina Lassus — Enzo Mari — Wolfgang Hintz — Andrea

Enrico Zanzi — Michael Graves — Il Bagno — Guido Venturini — Colorlink, Autori vari — Stefano Gi

ALESSI
· Designers & Products
· Progetti Speciali/Special Projects
· La storia/The history
· Libreria/Bookshop
· Worldwide Network
· News

7

STRICTLY FOR THE KIDS?

Giants of toy town, Lego **www.lego.com** and Playmobil **www.playmobil.com**, make fantastic use of available space, taking layout one step beyond 2-D. Interactive animation, snappy digitized sound effects, bold primary colors, and quirky perspective combine to create virtual cityscapes that little (and big!) visitors could spend half a lifetime exploring. Backed with added-value downloads and on-line buying, both layouts win.

154

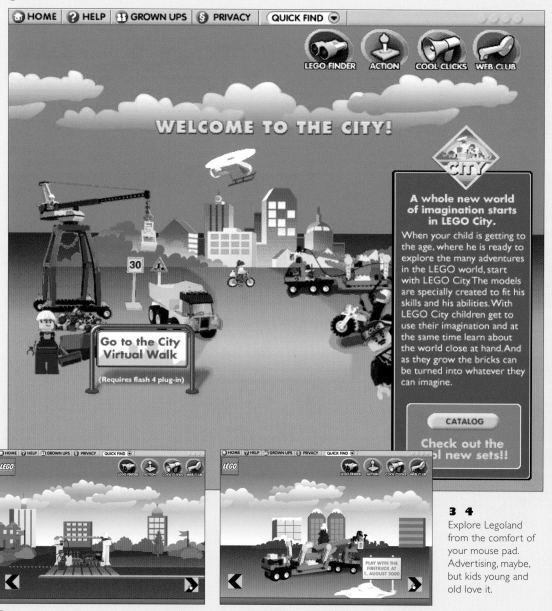

1 2
Coherence is the order of the day, and the neat buttons echo the style of Lego bricks.

3 4
Explore Legoland from the comfort of your mouse pad. Advertising, maybe, but kids young and old love it.

5

The official Homepage of

playmobil

Deutsch   English   Français

5 6 7 8 9
Somewhat less of a white-knuckle ride, Playmobil's enchanting Web site has the gentle air of charm that can't help but attract. Buttons made from Playmobil faces make for cute clicks.

6

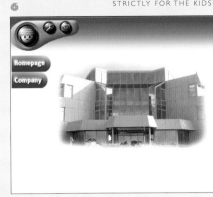

Homepage

Company

155

7

Homepage

NEU

Jetzt mit PLAYMOBIL® Online Shop
FunParks: Aktuelle Infos, Zahlen & Fakten

playmobil®

playmobil®
H@P

UNTERNEHMEN - PRODUKTE - SERVICE - FUNPARKS - SPIELE - ONLINE-SHOP

Postfach 12 60

QUICK FIND ▼

LEGO FINDER   ACTION   COOL CLICKS   WEB CLUB

Welcome to the
LEGO Worlds

LEGO

ROBORIDERS

8

playmobil®

Homepage

Product

Catalog

Fairy Tale

NEW!

3033 Princess with Magic Fountain
has peacock statue, options for gown or hoop skirt.

INFO

Attention!
Small parts may be swallowed.
Not recommended for children
under 3 years.

9

playmobil®

Homepage

Product

Catalog

Magic

3840 Dragon
3841 Dragon's Temple
3896 Fairy's Waterfall
3898 Tree Stump Goblin
3899 Hooded Rider

ADD-ONS

3896 Fairys Waterfall Rockies system compatible set features
detailed fairy with magic wand.

BRIT PACK

A nimated TV-like "screens" pop out of an otherwise black expanse at designer Paul Smith's Web site **www.paulsmith.co.uk**. Where most Web designers try hard to transcend the tight boundaries of a Web page, Smith's site has made a virtue of that very limitation, and the result is a compelling invitation.

Chinese bo
surfers sho

PAUL SMITH MEN
Spring/Summer 2000

For Spring/Summer 2000, Paul Smith creates an eclectic view of the global village. Recognising and celebrating contrasting cultures and combining them with a British touch that could only be Paul Smith.

High collared military jacket with contrast stitch detailing with three quarter length side split trousers

PAUL SMITH MEN s/s 2000

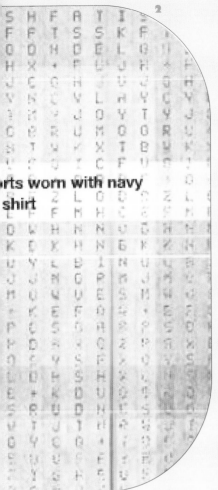

rts worn with navy

shirt

1
Find Paul Smith, and Britain's Union Jack flag won't be far away. Here, it heralds what is an unusual and highly interesting Web site. The music and movement in the opening animation give the feeling of being live at a fashion show—something difficult to achieve in print.

2 3 4 5 6 7 8
The clean side bars with the page numbers and icons straight from a 1970s' tape player make a strong layout feature that runs right through the site. Alphabets rendered as hieroglyphs give the backgrounds depth—likewise the blocky colors in the spring/ summer collection.

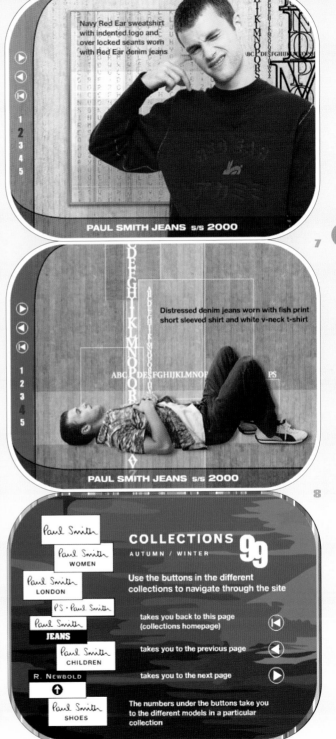

Navy Red Ear sweatshirt with indented logo and over locked seams worn with Red Ear denim jeans

PAUL SMITH JEANS s/s 2000

Distressed denim jeans worn with fish print short sleeved shirt and white v-neck t-shirt

PAUL SMITH JEANS s/s 2000

Chalk stripe suit with vibrant yellow insertions on the side seam, cuff and waistband with a top-stitched white t-shirt

PAUL SMITH MEN s/s 2000

Paul Smith
Paul Smith WOMEN
Paul Smith LONDON
P S · Paul Smith
Paul Smith JEANS
Paul Smith CHILDREN
R. NEWBOLD
Paul Smith SHOES

COLLECTIONS 99
AUTUMN / WINTER

Use the buttons in the different collections to navigate through the site

takes you back to this page (collections homepage)

takes you to the previous page

takes you to the next page

The numbers under the buttons take you to the different models in a particular collection

AIR HEAD

Loved and worn by millions, Dr. Martens AirWair footwear products feature in their very own Web site at **www.drmartens.com**. Contemporary layouts contain powerful visuals and innovative logos (with just a hint of retro) for a look that's funky yet familiar. And sunglasses **www.thesunglasscity.com** make the perfect partner.

1

158

2

3

1 2 3 4
Given their "alternative" pedigree, it is no wonder Dr. Martens boots translate perfectly to the Web. Clicking on individual footwear on the slide show brings up windows with greater detail. The layout is a pleasing blur of type and soft images.

4

Click on any image below for details

anarchy
blue gems
bucci
daggers
dmo
hobie
kids
killer loop
oakley
ray-ban
revo
smith
solar specs
vuarnet
other brands
links

 eye jacket

 fives

 frogskin

 mars

 romeo

 juliet

 minute

 straight jacket

 moon

 e wire

 zero 0.4sq sm

 m-frame heater

 square

Use the arrows to browse the range.
Click an image, to get the details

An archive of revolutionary designs that have walked their way into everyone's heart

UP

DOWN

Looking for
Con

other brands we carry & discount

SERENGETI
STYLE EYES
TIMBERLAND

Call Toll Free or E-Mail for Price Quotes

so many brands... so little time

5 6 7

There's that retro look again. Sunglass City's site draws attention to its product by using the graphic device of a featureless circle instead of a head.

159

7

GENUINE OAKLEYS

 Toll Free 1-888-822-RAYS

Your one stop shades shop since 1987

the **Sunglass City**

 100% genuine

anarchy
blue gems
bucci
daggers
dmo
hobie
kids
killer loop
oakley
ray ban
smith
solar specs
vuarnet
other brands
links

Chicks Dig 'Em

Oakley
the romeo

mission impossible shades?

enter here.

A n a r c h y ' s

The Torpedo

R a y B a n s

The Mystic

S m i t h s

The Toaster

Secure Server

✖ **order on-line !**

100% secure everyday

   VISA

THE BACKWARD GLANCE

What is it about ultra-new technology that generates such a powerful retro-oriented response from its users? The Web is stuffed with sites that hark back to happier times, all of them featuring 1950s-type styles and cartoon images of strong, serious men and stay-at-home women. Two excellent examples of this genre are Melinamade **www.melinamade.com** and the on-line past-times magazine, *Retro,* at **www.retroactive.com**.

A complete set of swatches is available in the Market.

List of All Fabrics...

FABRICS WALLPAPER ABOUT MARKET NEWS TIPS MAILINGS CONTACT

melinamade
Fabrics & Wallpaper

New Fabric

I'd rather be watching Swatch-O-Vision...

Yes, I read it in the melinamade news..

..as soon as I hang up, I'm going shopping at the melinamade market...

Melina has wallpapers? That's great!

YOUR SOURCE FOR FABULOUS FIFTIES FASHIO

1 2 3
Fantastic fifties' images set against period-styled type give Melinamade a look straight out of *Good Housekeeping* circa 1958. The image on the left doubles as a map. Swatch-o-vision (3) is a fun way to see fabrics.

THE MAGIC OF SW

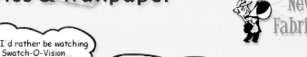

3

happy new year

4 5
Retro is an on-line magazine devoted to nostalgia. Sumptuous graphics lift the occasionally pedestrian designs straight off the screen.

161

RETRO™

table of contents

VISION

RETRO

5

in this **RETRO** *issue...*   **February 16, 2000**

First time here? Read all about RETRO magazine in our FAQ.
NEW: In February 2000, the Encyclopedia Britannica selected RETRO as one of the best sites on the Internet when reviewed for quality, accuracy of content, presentation and usability. You can now search Britannica directly from our table of contents page.

In June, 1999, RETRO went on hiatus and is currently on hold. Find out the details here.
Please note: Our Postcard Depot is up to date with scads of valentines, and people are exchanging information in our Backtalk board...so we're still alive!

RETRO'S
RED HOT
updates

Sign up for our update list and we'll keep you apprised of any new articles that we add to the RETRO site.
(We do not disclose this list to third parties. In other words, we serve no spam with our red hots.)

ALTERNATIVE TAKES

Web cams—live video pictures transmitted across the Net—were first used in weather monitoring systems and for other equally mundane tasks. It wasn't long however, before those with an eye for opportunity began to use them for increasingly esoteric purposes. Sex sites took the lead, and now there's television's worm's eye view of ordinary people's lives at Big Brother **www.bigbrother.com**.

1

by the people. for the people.
sitemap

WWW.BIGBROTHER.ORG
www.bigbrother.org

news/headlines
information
message board
archives
links
home

We're changing, mutating, evolving... soon to become the ultimate in websites informing you of how your individual rights are being violated. This site as of yet has not launched. Please check out our current goals and if you are interested in helping or just providing your two cents, subscribe to our mailing list on which we are begining to discuss direction and focus for the site as well as finding those among us who will be able to help.

If you think you can help with this, we are looking for looking for more brave souls who are willing volunteer their time to better the world we live in. We have two mailing lists you can join. One, THESITE, is a discussion forum for those interested in participating with the development of the website. The other, POLITICS, is for disscussion of how bigbrother is affecting you and yours. Send email to one of the following addresses to subscribe.

thesite-subscribe@bigbrother.org
politics-subscribe@bigbrother.org

Get a free guestbook at BigBrother.org

Site goals:
● To provide a place for news relating to privacy and human rights.
● To establish a repository for security and privacy related information and programs.
● To provide plain and simple editorial and help to understand the items listed above.

162

2

BIG BROTHER

HTTP://WWW.BIGBROTHER.COM

BIG BROTHER

HTTP://WWW.BIGBROTHER.COM

Bigbrother.com asks you to check out bigbrother.org they are an early stage freedom related site. looking for volunteers to help them in the fight against the oppresive bigbrother. (possibly bigbrother.com is that oppresive bigbrother?)

Looking for webcams! Many more webcams to come!
email us your favorite webcams to be included here. (note: we have received alot of adult content related camera request. we'll not put those up here.)

Here are the webcams from the "bigbrother house" - from CBS:

Check out the world famous JenniCam from www.jennicam.org

Follow the lives of 12 college students all living in the same dorm.

and the not quite as famous camgirl from www.acamgirl.com

1 | 2
Big Brother's Picasso-like site is a pleasing jumble of soft images and blueprint-like drawings. Its air of lopsided voyeurism is founded on type snipped from old newspapers and poison-pen letters.

3
For today's 15 minutes of fame, all that is needed is on-line space and a cheap video camera piping pictures directly onto the Web. Big Brother sports a selection of the better cams.

3

Award-winning Site Design, E-Commerce, and Custom Web-based Applications.

I'm Y2ok, You're Y2ok.

About us

Articles

Software

Contact

Over the past few months, many of our clients have asked us about the Y2K "readiness" of their Caravan-supplied web services. We're always happy to be able to tell them that we're Y2K ready. Still, the question has been raised often enough, that we thought it might be worthwhile to answer it briefly in this column.

First of all, let's say a few things about our standard servers. All of our servers are i586 and i686-class systems running the NetBSD operating system. We use the Apache webserver and the Stronghold SSL server. Many of our database-backed sites also rely on the PHP scripting language and the PostgreSQL ORDBMS.

To the best of our knowledge, all of the major software and hardware components in our systems are already fully Y2K ready. In Q3 of 1999, we will be conducting a thorough audit of all the Javascript and Perl scripts used on our sites to ensure trouble-free operation in the new millennium.

In addition, we have a very aggressive backup and data retention policy. Client data is backed up to DLT cartridges at least once each day. Databases are backed up three times a day. A duplicate set of backups is stored offsite twice a month.

All of our content creation and processing machines are Y2K compliant Macintosh PowerPCs running Mac OS 8.6. [Editor: Our designers note with glee that the Mac OS and most Macintosh applications can handle internally generated dates correctly all the way to the year 29,940. Sigh.]

Even though we are pretty confident that we will be free of significant Y2K problems, Caravan will be issuing special emergency procedures and contact points to all our clients in the month of December, just to be on the safe side. If you have any questions about our Y2K preparedness, please don't hesitate to contact us.

Note: Here are links to the individual Y2K statements for some of the software mentioned in this column:

NetBSD
Apache Server
Stronghold Server
PHP Scripting Language
PostgreSQL Relational Database
Apple Computer

Caravan in the News:

The melinamade fabrics site is featured in the May 99 issue of **Vogue** magazine. It was also selected as one of the "Great Websites for the 1950s" by **Encarta**.

Tea Time was highlighted in the Feb 99 issue of **Sunset** magazine.

Retro Magazine was a Project Cool sighting on January 18, 1999 and a USA Today Hot Site on Jan 26!

The San Jose Mercury recommended the John Denver Remembered Video in their "Just Go" Holiday Guide on December 15.

WIRED magazine did a full-page article on the melinamade site in Nov 98. It was also positively reviewed in Netscape's Netcenter (8|8) on Nov 2nd.

Yahoo Internet Life gave the James Dean Memorial Gallery site a "Yippee Yahooey" rating for its design in Nov 98.

Recent work:

James Dean Gallery

Portable Batch System

Melinamade Fabrics

Work in Progress:

Lenny of New York

Cat Carney Ecological Fashions

MRJ Technology Solutions

ExtremelyModern.com

5

4 5
Caravan www. caravan.com is a company specializing in graphic design for the Web. Naturally, the layout of its own site is super-stylish.

SHELLING OUT

Egg **www.egg.com** offers e-finance management for the Web age. There's no corporate identity other than the stark white backgrounds and simple "egg" logo. Instead, egg's layouts feature cut-out "customers" with the right kind of lifestyles. You surf, recognize yourself as a potential egg-head, and sign up on-line for financial advice. The power-packed information is set in smart and well-managed type.

1 2 3
Money-matters sold on style—after all, what could be more boring than managing investments?

2

1

164

egg: Individual Money Matters

A personal loan
that suits you.

You could take a repayment break, reduce your repayments or pay off your loan early - all penalty free. And our rates are competitive - just 9.9% APR when you borrow £10,000 or more. Why not apply online today?

More Info

Wednesday 19 July 2000 | News from Egg | Click here to

Egg Investments
PEP not performing? Compare it to over 120 funds in the Egg PEP Centre. Huge discounts until 31 July.

Mind Blowing
Now a low 2.5% APR for 6 months if you transfer your balances to Egg Card. Blown away?

▶ More Info

Egg Shopping
With over 100 special offers and 2% cash back when you buy with your Egg Card, click here to start shopping at Egg.

with Deutsche Asset Management

Aberdeen
Source: Lipper offer to bid net income reinvested to 28/04/00

▶ Shopping ▶ Apply Now ▶ Products ▶ Your Account
▶ Investments ▶ Egg-free zone ▶ Contact Us ▶ Site Help

Site Contents ⬍
go

---

egg: Individual Money Matters

We
Egg Inve

Why pay up to 5%
discounts on over
are discounted by

● For ISAs a
● To transfer

**To start investing
remember, all yo
guaranteed!**

SPECIAL OFFER:
Seminar, visit ou

▶ Site Map

How do
started.

with Egg Invest
a two minute ov

---

egg:

Mind

Now a low **2.5% AP**
transfer your balance

Apply Now

Benefits
**Save whenever you spend
Card. Transfer your card ba
online. Apply online
for a decision in
seconds.
Check out the
benefits now.**

egg:

3

Log off

e to

Egg Investments offers huge
ing managers, the majority of which

e <u>Fund Supermarket</u>
Centre.

<u>Savings Account</u> and
ns with Egg are secure - that's

Motley Fool Online Investments
to find out more.

▸ ISA/PEP Centre

Learn.

Everything you need
to know if you're new
to investing.

My Organiser.

Manage your
investment portfolio
online.

165

4
Each of the icons on
the carrier bag is a
hyperlink to financial
products.

5
There's even an
informal chat page
tailored to those tired
of wheeler-dealing.

ving

ou
wn away?

Shop

B on 12 bottles
Only £39.99
xtra bottles

Flexible Loans

Competitive rates -
just 9.9% APR when
you borrow £10,000
or more. Apply
online today.

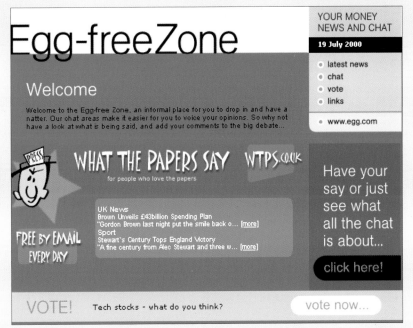

Egg-freeZone

YOUR MONEY
NEWS AND CHAT

19 July 2000

- latest news
- chat
- vote
- links

- www.egg.com

Welcome

Welcome to the Egg-free Zone, an informal place for you to drop in and have a
natter. Our chat areas make it easier for you to voice your opinions. So why not
have a look at what is being said, and add your comments to the big debate...

WHAT THE PAPERS SAY WTPS.co.uk
for people who love the papers

FREE BY EMAIL
EVERY DAY

UK News
Brown Unveils £43billion Spending Plan
"Gordon Brown last night put the smile back o... [more]
Sport
Stewart's Century Tops England Victory
"A fine century from Alec Stewart and three w... [more]

Have your
say or just
see what
all the chat
is about...

click here!

VOTE!   Tech stocks - what do you think?   vote now...

NAME FAME

It is conceivable that companies such as Gucci **www.gucci.it**, Tiffany **www.tiffany.com**, and Cartier **www.cartier.fr**, already benchmarks of style and elegance, don't need to prove the point on the Web. They do, however, with smooth, sophisticated layouts straight from the pages of a glossy magazine. Inspop **www. inspop.com** sports a design which, while not as sophisticated, is neat, tidy, and color-coordinated.

TIFFANY & CO.

Tiffany & Co. welcomes you to our Web site. Click on the titles above for information about America's house of design since 1837. At your convenience, please visit us at a location near you. For shopping, click here.

THE COLLECTION   GUCCI CULTURE   INVESTOR CENTER   GUCCI CONTACT

GUCCI

1 2 3

Established names putting the others to shame. You can look but you can't touch the beauty that graces these sites.

inspop.com

about us   insurers   **press information**   **terms & conditions**   **privacy policy**

motor

home

travel

health

pets

life

help

contact

Hello and welcome to inspop.com - the web site able to give you a range of independent quotes from leading insurance providers.

Our aim is to speed up and simplify the process of buying insurance, by helping you to find the best deal.

Just give us your details once and within seconds we'll give you a range of quotes ranked in order of premium. We'll also give you the small print, so you can compare value for money quickly and easily.

We don't charge commission and can guarantee you the same prices as going direct to your provider. Just choose the best policy for you and buy online with either Mastercard or Visa.

Although we can offer the full inspop service for Travel Insurance, we are currently resolving technical hitches on Home and Motor insurance. We can offer Home insurance quotes from Hiscox, the high value home insurer and Budget (who will provide a quote within 24 hours). We apologise for this situation and are doing every thing possible to establish the full service at the earliest opportunity.

Please read our terms and conditions and privacy policy before buying from our site.

Enter our email competition...

Please select the type of insurance you require from the menu on the left or if you're an existing customer, log in below

login

Renew the way you buy insurance with inspop.com

---

4 5 6 7

On-line insurance company Inspop's purple-blue color scheme won't be to everyone's taste, but the layout is neat, there are plenty of easily-accessible icons, and although the text measure is a little wide, it is legible.

5

 home insurance

We have a number of companies signed up to offer home insurance an quote engines directly to our website. We hope that you bear with us d get a quotation from Hiscox Insurance and the Budget Group of Compa also be quoting for Prudential Insurance and RIAS.

To make sure we get the most competitive quotes, we need some deta

To save time please confirm the following:

General

- I/we permanently reside at the property.

7

? help

What is the benefit of using inspop.com over going direct?

We know from our research that, on average, people get up to
This means calling five different companies and giving the sar
benefit of going direct without the hassle of calling around an

What makes inspop.com different to other Insurance web s

Being completely independent, inspop.com is working on you
leading Insurance providers. The new site offers a revolutiona
providing a fast-track service for all your insurance needs - sav

Is it cheaper than going direct?

Because inspop.com has secured guarantees from all its insu
site you can rest safe in the knowledge that you are getting th

How long does it take?

Just a few seconds after giving us your details, you will get a
a comparison table, to help you decide on the best policy. All
enter your credit card details. You will then receive a referenc

We estimate that the whole process won't take more than 15
to shop for the best insurance deal.

6

SMART ART

Worthy-renowned art materials manufacturer Caran d'Ache www.carandache.ch has created a glorious site packed with richly colored images of pencils, paint palettes, and the like. Daler-Rowney www.daler-rowney.com has followed suit, choosing a layout that makes use of crisp white backgrounds to complement images of its art materials.

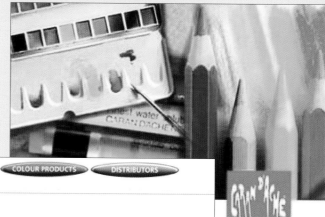

2

| HISTORY | LUXURY PRODUCTS | NEWS | COLOUR PRODUCTS | DISTRIBUTORS |

History

1 2 3
Caran d'Ache's beautiful logo sits well with colorful images of pencils, and the delightful buttons on the home page are highly reminiscent of watercolor paints in their box.

Caran d'Ache is the Russian word for "pencil" and was th

French painter, caricaturist and designer, Emmanuel P

Moscow in 1859 and died in Paris in 1909. He was the g

the Great Army and consequently liked a lot of military flo

glorified the Napoleon epopee. He contributed to the news

CARAN d'ACHE

OF SWITZERLAND

Soft drop-shadows
behind cut-out
images of art
materials, all on
eye-catching white
backgrounds, set off
Daler-Rowney's site
perfectly.

BRUSHES

Cryla Brushes
Designed for acrylic painting. The Cryla brush range covers a wide variety of shapes and sizes. All brushes have natural look fibres which provide high resilience and durability, and each brush is fitted with a seamless ferrule and a unique marbled handle.

Series C10 — Series C10 Short Handle Round
CODE 204 010*
A brush with excellent spring and pointing characteristics, good for detail work as well as fluid 'watercolour' applications.
Sizes: 000, 00, 0, 1, 2, 3, 4, 5, 6, 7, 8, 9, 10, 12, 14.
Size 000 = 204 810 000

Series C15 — Series C15 Short Handle Wash One Stroke
CODE 204 015*
This square edged brush has excellent colour carrying capacity and allows for good paint flow. Ideal for laying down large areas of flat colour.
Sizes: 3mm, 6mm, 10mm, 12mm, 19mm, 25mm.

Series C20 — Series C20 Long Handle Round
CODE 204 020*
Can be used for touching in small areas, fine detailing and for applying well thinned paint.
Sizes: 1, 2, 3, 4, 6, 8, 10, 12.

5

169

DALER~ROWNEY   LOST? Index

7

PRINTING COLOURS

Screen and Fabric Printing Colour
Acrylic Based
Sizes: 60ml jar **CODE 143 060** ◆ ◆ ◆
Sizes: 454ml jar **CODE 143 454** ◆ ◆ ◆

Daler-Rowney Screen & Fabric
Printing Colours may be used on either
fabric or paper and can be applied
through screens or with brushes,
sponges etc. Water soluable while still
moist all equipment can be used straight from the jar of blended made
lighter or transparent by use of the extender medium or made opaque br adding white.

Fixing
Colour can be fixed to fabric
by ironing on the reverse side once the
colour is dry.

Fixing Times
Times will vary. Allow 3 minutes per
0.1sq metre for cotton, tp 10 minutes
per 0.1sq metre for silk.

Fabrics
Coton, silk, linen and other natural
fibres can be screen printed, but
coarse fibre fabric will obviously
obscure fine detail in design. All fabrics
should be washed and ironed **before**
printing. Daler-Rowney Screen & Fabric
printing colours will not affect the finish
or the handle of fabrics on which they
are printed.

Cleaning of Screens
1. Keep the ink moist.
2. Wash with soap and water.
3. Dry colour can normally be removed
   with warm water or finally with
   menthylated spirit.

THIRST FOR COLOR

Stark black backgrounds have an unsettling quality that is at once interesting and stimulating. The world-renowned brewer Guinness **www.guinness.ie** makes a virtue of its monochrome identity, using bold sans serif type, occasional use of color, and a certain amount of street cachet to carry what is in fact a very simple design. Three cheers, too, for Absolut vodka's **www.absolut.com**, which is certain to make heads spin!

170

WELCOME TO GUINN

WHERE ARE YOU
SITTING ?

USA   CANADA   GREAT BRITAIN   IRELAND   CONT
AFRICA   ASIA   AUSTRALASIA   LATIN AMERICA

GUINNESS® WELCOME TO ONLINE REFRESHME

▶ **WHERE DO YOU WANT TO DRINK TODAY?**

Dive in to the GUINNESS® Little Black Book – a guide to some of the best of Br... you fancy venturing further afield, we've got everything you need to know for a break in Dublin!

▶ **PLAY THE GAME**

Play 'Don't Lose Your Bottle', the brilliant new game from Guinness. It's free, it's online and not only do we have loads of GUINNESS® to give away but you could also win a fantastic MP3 watch.

WHERE DO YOU WANT TO DRINK TODAY?

CLICK FOR
UK / DUBLIN?

ENJOY THE
ART

GASTROPOD GAME
GASTROPOD SCREENSAVER
SURFER STUFF
SWIMBLACK AD
ANTICIPATION SCREENSAVER

FANCY A CHANGE? TERMS & CONDITIONS

TASTE THE
DRINK

HISTORY OF GUINNESS
3 TYPES
DID YOU KNOW?
STEP-BY-STEP BREWING GUIDE
BREW YOUR OWN
HOPSTORE VISITORS' CENTRE

LIVE THE
LIFE

WHERE DO YOU WANT TO DRINK TODAY?
DUBLIN GUIDE
GREAT BRITISH PUBS
THE DON'T LOSE YOUR BOTTLE GAME
THE GILROY CLASSIC COLLECTION

2

1 2
Guinness dilutes its design with restrained colors. The "blocky," geometric layout is softened by the use of the signature in striking scarlet.

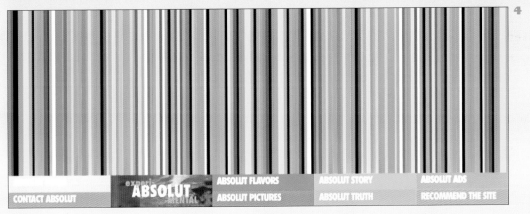

4

3 4 5
Heineken's corporate green fizzes all over **www.heineken.com** (3) while colorless Absolut vodka (**www.absolut.com**) shows clear vision by splashing color throughout its site.

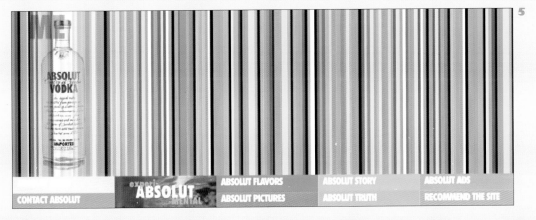

5

AB FAB

Bastions of style, both *Elle* **www.elle.com** and *Vogue* **www.vogue.com** fail to make a statement on the Web—unless a tousled and dated layout is what they're currently pushing. *Elle* wins, if only because of the crisp white background and contemporary use of light sans serif type, but there is little to draw the eye. *Vogue* fails miserably with a color scheme straight out of a club magazine and clichéd Web gadgetry.

1 2
The cut-out fashion shots on white backdrops save an otherwise mediocre site.

172

2

VOGUE.COM

vogue.com presents
CHANEL
cruise 2001
reserve your favorite looks now

collection
central
the models

2000 2000
fall spring

Vogue's clumsy, dated site stuffed with Web clichés takes an age to download and repulses the eye when it eventually arrives. The pop-up menus are horrible, the type is unreadable, and the color scheme unappealing.

3

4

173

VOGUE

NEW TO VOGUE.COM?
Wednesday, June 14

collections
- CRUISE 2001
- FALL 2000
- VIDEOS
- SPRING 2000

accessories

CHANEL cruise 20

NEW YORK SPRING 2000 READY-TO-WEAR COLLECTIONS

COLLECTIONS | CELEBRITIES | BACKSTAGE

new york designers ⬍ GO

10 MOST WANTED LOOKS

oscar de la renta | donna karan

michael kors | ralph lauren

tuleh | marc jacobs

new york wrap-up

The first clear trends for Spring/Summer 2000 emerged as the New York collections wrapped up on Saturday. Under the tents at Bryant Park and elsewhere around the city, fashion week was dominated by luxury--a stark contrast to the strict utilitarian looks of seasons past. Embroidery, ...on are the keywords ...of the new ...te, very feminine ...se, coral and ivory, ...and graphic prints, ...ys. At the same time, ...etic has emerged, ...set style of the late ...Denim, often accented ...d paillette trimming, ...ong influence for next ...hcoats in lightweight, ...ced fabrics were ...g from slinky cocktail ...eather skirts and ...h sorbet shades. The ...rs have addressed ...s of modern women, ...erfect dress for a ...and a glamorous ...b-hopping. So tighten ...aps on your Manolos ...n is in fashion this

...y York Fashion Week ...or view each designer's ...licking below:

...signer ⬍ GO

g 2000 ready-to-wear collection coverage

york | london | milan | paris

st comprehensive guide to the shows — ever!

-WANTED LOOKS	new york ⬍ GO
DAILY DISH	sunday 9.12 ⬍ GO
DESIGNERS	SEE DESIGNER LIST
CELEBRITIES	new york ⬍ GO
:STAGE/MODELS	new york ⬍ GO

HIGH TECH

Who else but Swedes could be responsible for the ultra-blue Volvo site, **www.volvo.com.** Oozing authority, the ice-cool world map stamps Volvo's corporate identity on a global scale. Meanwhile, Audi **www.audi.com** uses sweeping lines and alabaster tones to complement what it perceives as its firmly upmarket image.

I

2

174

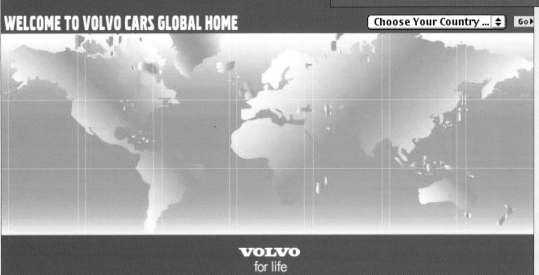

1 2 3 4
Volvo's novel spotlight feature is used to highlight vehicle details. Type is an instant pointer to the car company's corporate identity, and the site as a whole makes for a coherent experience —except for the ugly country pop-up menu!

3

4

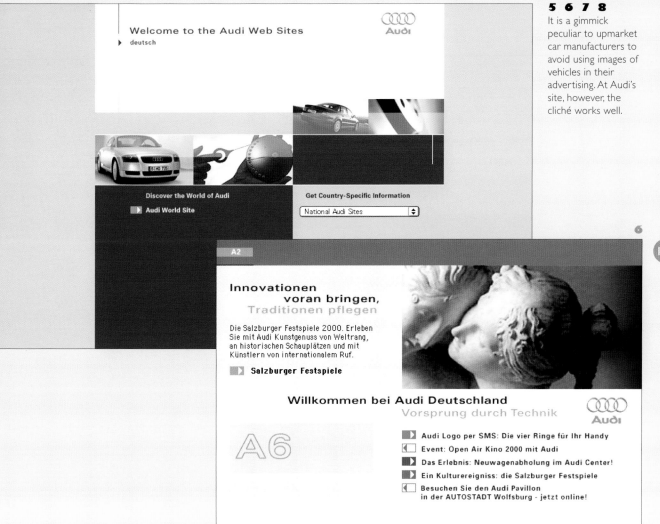

5 6 7 8
It is a gimmick
peculiar to upmarket
car manufacturers to
avoid using images of
vehicles in their
advertising. At Audi's
site, however, the
cliché works well.

6

175

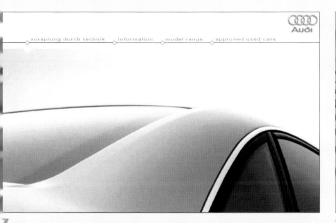

7   8

TECH SPEC

The Web is used to sell everything from high-tech computer equipment to washing machines, but when companies take the trouble to create competent layouts like these, the results are equally stylish. Umax www.umax.com has chosen "traditional" tabs, icons, and image maps. Zanussi www.zanussi.com has, meanwhile, opted for slick artwork over sophisticated layouts.

1 2
Though a "traditional" Web layout, the Umax design features a smart color scheme and practical image maps.

3
Descriptive icons arc around the central, attractively rendered image.

ZANUSSI

HOME

ABOUT
ZANUSSI

DESIGN &
INNOVATION

PRODUCTS

GALLERY

THE FUTURE
TODAY

MAIN EVENTS

SITE MAP

THE FUTURE
i
HERE

D E S I G N
&
INNOVATION

ECONOMY

Live-in exploits off-peak rates for maximum economy. It
will also avoid overloading the electrical system at times of
peak family demand.

4 5 6 7 8
You'd be forgiven for
mistaking Zanussi's
gorgeous washing
machine for a digital
camera! The
company's site mixes
retro cartoons with
high-tech,
sophisticated layouts,
creating a site that
demands attention.

6

ZANUSSI   D E S I G N & **INNOVATION**   HOME

POWER
TO CLEAN
THE DIRTIEST
POTS AND
PANS

WRD

SID
SUPER INTENSITY
DISPENSER

TOP PERFORMANCE   USEFUL SOLUTIONS   THE FUTURE TODAY   1/3 ▶

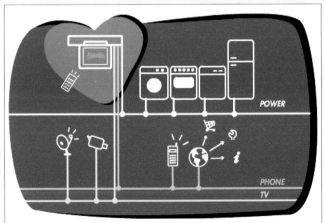

POWER

PHONE
TV

7

February 22nd 12:55 alarm: fridge, door open

i ✉ 📱   ← →

8

UNDER CONSTRUCTION

Surf the Web for more than a few minutes and you will soon arrive at a site "under construction." Occasionally, this is genuine downtime while the Web master responsible makes adjustments. More often, it is because someone has decided a Web-presence is a good idea, but no one has the skills to turn it into reality. Not so, Saatchi and Saatchi **www.saatchila.com**. When the arch image manipulator's Web site goes under construction, they put a stylish offering in its place.

1

Today our commodities are ideas.

Saatchi & S
Gone are th
We are, in
As such, we
resources a
reflect this
revitalizing
In the mean
contact us,
We're alway

contact@saatchila.com
310 | 214 – 6085
310 | 214 – 6160 fax

2

NDORRSGAPLESOS ANGELES NEW YORK SYDNEY MELBOURNE
NG KONG SINGAPORE WELLINGTON AUCKLAND DUBAI RIYADH FIJI

1. BRUTAL SIMPLICITY OF THOUGHT

When developing global advertising it is easier to complicate than to simplify

SINGAPORE

Advertising that communicates a simple message enters the brain quicker and stays longer

38 CLUB STREET

Brutal simplicity of thought is therefore a painful necessity

SINGAPORE 069418

TEL. +65 227 3381

BACK

1 2 3
Interesting use of type builds a complete layout that lifts Saatchi's site out of the ordinary.

ONDONSPAINLOS ANGELESNEW YORKSYDNEYMELBOURNE
ONG KONGSINGAPOREWELLINGTONAUCKLANDDUBAIRIYADHFIJI

3

London
Pentagram

Pentagram
Architecture

Recent Work
Industrial Design

Pentagram

4 5 6 7
Despite its tired logo, the clean layout of Pentagram's temporary "downtime" site **www.pentagram.com** was smart and spare—a perfect showcase for the company's work. The manageable type measure was refreshingly legible.

Diba
This is startup company with hardware and software architecture that allows development of simple, accessible and inexpensive computing devices. Our product designs for <u>Diba</u> communicate the company's vision and technology in fun, exciting and useful ways.
More images from this program

B&W Loudspeakers
The dramatic 800 Matrix series is that we have designed since 1974 audio equipment.

What We Do

- Home
- Who We Are
- Ideas
- Exchange

Recent Work   Clients   Pentagram Publications   Site Index

We offer design services in the following areas and welcome assignments that require a mix of these capabilities

Kenwood
The Compact Travel Steam Iron S that incorporates the features of a dual voltage appliance has a remov integral with the handle and allows

citi

Graphic Design
The creation of any and all of the visual facets of an organization related to the projection of its identity: printed and on-screen communications, technical and promotional information; publications for products, sales and finance; books, magazines and newspapers; the form and labeling of packaging; and integrated sign systems and environmental graphics.
Recent Work

Industrial Design
The design and development of products, merchandise, packaging and equipment for domestic, commercial and industrial use and consumption: conceptualization and model-making; definition of production details and processes; and research and management of manufacturing and marketing resources.
Recent Work

GLOSSARY

8-bit Of display monitors or digital images—the allocation of eight data bits to each pixel, producing a display or image of 256 grays or colors (a row of eight bits can be written in 256 different combinations: 0000000, 00000001, 10000001, 00111100, and so on).

24-bit color The allocation of 24 bits of memory to each pixel, giving a possible screen display of 16.7 million colors (a row of 24 bits can be written in 16.7 million different combinations of 0s and 1s). Twenty-four bits are required for CMYK separations—eight bits for each.

absolute path The path, or route, taken to locate a file by starting at the highest level and searching through each directory (or folder) until the file is found. The path is spelled out by listing each directory en route.

absolute URL A complete address, or "uniform resource locator" (URL), which takes you to a specific location in a Web site rather than to the home page of the site. An absolute URL will contain the full file path to the page document location on the host server, for example: "http://yoursite.com/extrainfo/about you/yourhouse.htm."

active hyperlink A currently selected word or button which forms a link to another location, often differentiated from other links on the same page by a different color.

ActiveX Microsoft's proprietary technology for creating interactive Web pages. ActiveX controls are not platform-independent and are mainly supported only in Microsoft Windows environments.

Afterburner Proprietary file compression software for compressing and delivering Macromedia Director film strips on the Internet.

AIFF (*abb.*: Audio Interchange File Format) Macintosh sound file format. PCs running Windows 9.x can play .aiff files.

aliasing The term describing the jagged appearance of bitmapped images or fonts either when the resolution is insufficient or when they have been enlarged. This is caused by the pixels—which are square with straight sides—making up the image becoming visible.

ALT tag Explanatory text displayed in place of a picture. Useful for Web users who have turned off graphics loading or who are using text-only browsers. ALT tags can also serve as explanations for images designated as links. PNG images do not need ALT tags as they already have a text identifier.

anchor A hyperlink that takes you to another part of the same Web page, rather than to a sub-page or another site elsewhere on the Web.

antialias/antialiasing A technique of optically eliminating the jagged effect of bitmapped images or text reproduced on low-resolution devices such as monitors. This is achieved by adding pixels of an in-between tone—the edges of the object's color are blended with its background by averaging the density of the range of pixels involved. Antialiasing is also sometimes employed to filter texture maps, such as those used in 3-D applications, to prevent moiré patterns.

applet Mini-programs embedded in HTML documents which provide animations, hit counters, rollover buttons, etc. Applets are written in a scripting language.

ASCII (*pron.*: asskee) Acronym for the American Standard Code for Information Interchange, a code which assigns a number to 256 letters, numbers, and symbols (including carriage returns and tabs) which can be typed on a keyboard. ASCII is the cross-platform, computer-industry-standard, text-only file format.

attribute (**1**) A characteristic of an HTML tag which is identified alongside the tag in order to describe it.

attribute (**2**) The specification applied to a character, box, or other item. Character attributes include font, size, style, color, shade, scaling, kerning, etc.

banner An image on a Web page, usually at the top, which deliberately attracts attention, generally for advertising purposes.

baud In data transmission by modem, the number of signal changes transmitted per second.

baud rate The speed at which a modem transmits data, or the number of "events" it can handle per second. Often used to describe the transmission speed of data itself but, since a single event can contain two or more bits, data speed is more correctly expressed in "bits per second" (bps).

binary code The computer code, using 1 or 0, which is used to represent a character or instruction. For example, the binary code 01100010 represents a lower-case "b."

binary file A file which is described in binary code rather than text. Binary files typically hold pictures, sounds, or a complete application program.

binary system Numbering system which uses two digits, 0 and 1, as distinct from the decimal system of 0–9.

bit Acronym for binary digit, the smallest piece of information a computer can use. A bit is expressed as one of two values, which can be a 1 or a 0, on or off, something or nothing, negative or positive, small or large, etc. Each alphabet character requires eight bits (called a "byte") to store it.

bit density The number of bits occupying a particular area or length—per inch of magnetic tape, for example.

bit depth Describes the number of bits assigned to each pixel on a monitor, scanner, or image file. One-bit, for example, will produce only black and white (the bit is either on or off), whereas 8-bit will generate 256 grays or colors (256 is the maximum number of permutations of a string of eight 1s and 0s), and 24-bit will produce 16.7 million colors (256 × 256 × 256).

bit map/bitmap Strictly speaking any text character or image comprised of dots. A bit map is a "map" of "bits" describing the complete collection of the bits that represent the location and binary state (on or off) of a corresponding set of items, such as pixels, which are required to form an image, such as on a display monitor.

bit rate The speed at which data is transmitted across communications channels, measured in bits per second (bps). Sometimes erroneously referred to as baud rate.

bitmapped font A font in which the characters are made up of dots, or pixels, as distinct from an outline font, which is drawn from "vectors." Bitmapped fonts generally accompany PostScript®, "Type 1" fonts and are used to render the fonts' shape on screen (they are sometimes called "screen" fonts). To draw the shape accurately on screen, your computer must have a bitmap installed for each size (they are also called "fixed-size" fonts), although this is not necessary if you have ATM installed, as this uses the outline, or "printer" version of the font (the file that your printer uses in order to print it). True-Type® fonts are "outline" and thus do not require a bitmapped version.

bitmapped graphic An image made up of dots, or pixels, and usually generated by "paint" or "image-editing" applications, as distinct from the "vector" images of "object-oriented" drawing applications.

body One of the main structures of an HTML document, falling between the header and the footer.

bookmark Favorite pages on the Web can be bookmarked by your browser, which stores links to sites or pages marked in this way. Invoking such a link takes you directly to the bookmarked page.

Boolean Named after G. Boole, a 19th-century English mathematician, Boolean is used to describe a shorthand for logical computer operations, such as those which link values ("and," "or," "not," "nor," etc., called "Boolean operators"). For example, the search of a database could be refined using Boolean operators, such as in "book and recent or new but not published." "Boolean expressions" compare two values and come up with the result ("return") of either "true" or "false," which are each represented by 1 and 0. In 3D applications, Boolean describes the joining or removing of one shape from another.

button see hyperlink

burn To convert a file from an uncompressed to a compressed format for use specifically with Internet Web browsers.

byte A single group made up of eight bits (0s and 1s) processed as one unit. It is possible to configure eight 0s and 1s in only 256 different permutations. Thus a byte can represent any value between 0 and 255—the maximum number of ASCII characters for example, one byte being required for each.

cascading style sheet (**CSS**) Similar to an ordinary style sheet in a DTP program, a CSS is used to make styling changes to a single piece of text or throughout a Web page. A document of styles can be applied across the pages of a site to maintain consistent design. An internal style sheet is one applied to the text of a single Web page, whereas an external style sheet is applied to any or all of the pages of an entire site. Internal style sheets may be either embedded or inline. The first is a group of styles in the HTML heading of a Web document that applies to every associated HTML tag throughout the document. The second are inserted into the tag pair of a single style within the document and affect only the text between the tags. External style sheets are linked or imported. A linked style sheet is a document containing the styles you want to apply; this is done, using a <LINK> tag, to selected pages. Imported style sheets work in a similar way in that they feature a document of styles linked to Web pages, but they also feature local styles that are applied in much the same way as internal style sheets. CSS supports the usual pixel or percentage measurements of HTML, but measurements can be in points, picas, centimeters, ems, and so on. This allows precision measuring an order of magnitude better than what was previously available. Colors, however, are handled poorly in the current CSS1 standard, with only 16 colors available from the World Wide Web Consortium's standard color palette. CSS is not HTML, but uses a similar coding system. This code combines with HTML tags and is interpreted by compatible browsers as a homogenized whole.

cell A space containing information in the rows or columns of a table.

cell padding The space between cells in a table.

cell spacing The number of pixels between cells in a table.

centered Type which is centered in its measure, as distinct from ranged (aligned) left or right.

CGI (*abb.*: common gateway interface) Software required to handle data submitted online by Web users when responding to forms and other requests for information. When the visitor clicks the submit button, a CGI script (or simply "script") is invoked on a special forms server provided by the ISP; this processes the submitted data and generates a response of some kind, which is transmitted to the visitor. For forms to work your ISP must support CGI scripting.

CGI script An applet which is run on the server rather than downloaded to, and run on, a visitor's computer.

character On a computer, any single letter, number, punctuation mark, or symbol represented by 8 bits (1 byte), including invisible characters such as "space," "return," and "tab."

Character Shape Player (**CSP**) Software, contained within a Web browser, which plays back the shape of characters in a Web page.

character/text mode Of Web browsers, those which can display text data only and which cannot display graphics without the assistance of a "helper" application. Even graphics-savvy browsers allow a preference for operating in character mode, which many users prefer due to the increased speed—although they inevitably miss out since it is common for much of the text on Web pages to be transmitted as images.

chatterbots The term given to software "helpers" that give advice and explain local etiquette in interactive environments—such as chat rooms—on the Web.

child (**object**) An object linked hierarchically to another object (its "parent"). For example, if a "child" box is placed within—or linked to—a "parent" box, when the latter is moved, the child—and all its "grandchildren"!—move with it, retaining their relative positions and orientation. This enables manipulation of complex structures, particularly in 3D applications.

chroma The intensity, or purity, of a color; thus its degree of saturation.

clickable map/image An invisible shape sur-

184

rounding a graphic on a Web page that serves as a "button" which, when clicked, will take you to another page or Web site.

closed file A file which does not have an access path, thus preventing you from reading from or writing to it.

CLUT Acronym for "color lookup table," a preset table of colors (to a maximum of 256 colors) which the operating system uses when in 8-bit mode. CLUTS are also attached to individual images saved in 8-bit "indexed" mode—that is, when an application converts a 24-bit image (one with millions of colors) to 8-bit, it draws up a table ("index") of up to 256 of the most frequently used colors in the image (the total number of colors depends on where the image will be viewed—Mac, Windows or Web, for example). If a color in the original image does not appear in the table, the application chooses the closest one or simulates it by "dithering" available colors in the table.

codec Acronym for "compressor/decompressor" which describes the technique used to rapidly compress and decompress sequences of images, such as those used for QuickTime and AVI movies.

color depth The number of bits required to define the color of each pixel. For example, only one bit is required to display a black-and-white image (it is either on or off), whereas an 8-bit image can display either 256 grays or 256 colors; and a 24-bit image displays 16.7 million colors—eight bits each for red green and blue (256 × 256 × 256).

color library An application support file that contains predefined colors. These may be the application's default colors, colors defined by you, or other predefined color palettes or tables.

color-management system (**CMS**) The name given to a method devised to provide accuracy and consistency of color representation across all devices in the color-reproduction chain—scanners, monitors, printers, image-setters and so on. Typical CMSs include the ones defined by the International Color Consortium (ICC), Kodak's Digital Science Color Management System, Apple's ColorSync, and Microsoft's ICM.

color model The method of defining or modifying color. Although there are many proprietary color models, such as PANTONE®, FOCOLTONE, TRUMATCH, TOYO, and DIC, the two generic models are those based on the way light is transmitted—the "additive" and "subtractive" color models. The additive color model is used, for example, in computer monitors, which transmit varying proportions of red, green, and blue (RGB) light, which we interpret as different colors. By combining the varying intensities of RGB light, we can simulate the range of colors found in nature. When 100 percent values of all three are combined, we perceive white; and if there is no light, we see nothing or, rather, black. The subtractive color model is based on the absorption (i.e., subtraction) and reflection of light. Printing inks are an example of this—if you subtract 100 percent values of either red, green, or blue from white light, you create cyan, magenta, or yellow.

color table A predefined table, or "index," of colors used to determine a specific color model—for example, for converting an image to CMYK. A color table, or "CLUT," also describes the palette of colors used to display an image.

comment tag Two or three words "attached" to an image that help to explain it for the benefit of Web surfers who prefer not to download graphics or who use text-only browsers.

compression The technique of rearranging data so that it either occupies less space on disk or transfers faster between devices or on communication lines. Different kinds of compression techniques are employed for different kinds of data—applications, for example, must not lose any data when compressed, whereas photographic images and movies can tolerate a certain amount of data loss. Compression methods which do not lose data are referred to as "lossless," whereas "lossy" is used to describe methods in which some data is lost. Movies and animations employ techniques called "codecs" (compression/decompression). There are many proprietary utilities for compressing data. Typical compression formats for images are LZW (lossless), JPEG, and GIF (both

lossy), the latter two commonly being used for files transmitted across the Internet.

cookie A small piece of information deposited in your Web browser (thus on your hard drive) by a WWW site, storing such things as custom page settings or even personal information about you, such as your address or your password for that site.

cross-platform The term applied to software, multimedia titles, or anything else (such as floppy disks) that will work on more than one computer platform—that is, those which run different operating systems, such as the Macintosh OS or Microsoft Windows.

data Although strictly speaking the plural of "datum," meaning a piece of information, "data" is now used as a singular noun to describe—particularly in the context of computers—more or less anything that can be stored or processed, whether it be a single bit, a chunk of text, an image, audio, and so on.

data bits A term used in data transmission to distinguish bits that contain the data being transmitted from bits that give instructions on how the data is to be transmitted.

database Information stored on a computer in a systematic fashion, and thus retrievable. This generally refers to files where you store any amount of data in separate but consistent categories (called "fields") for each type of information such as names, addresses, and telephone numbers. The electronic version of a card index system (each card is called a "record"), databases are constructed with applications called "database managers," which allow you to organize information any way you like.

descender The part of a lower case character that extends below the baseline of the x-height, as in the letters p, q, j, g, y.

differential letterspacing The spacing of each letter according to its individual width.

digit (**1**) Any numeral from 0 to 9.

digit (**2**) A printer's symbol ("ornament") depicting a hand with a pointing finger. Also known as a "hand," "fist," or "index."

digital Anything operated by or created from

information or signals represented by binary digits—such as in a digital recording. Distinct from analog, in which information is represented by a physical variable (in a recording, this may be via the grooves in a vinyl platter).

digital data Information stored or transmitted as a series of 1s and 0s ("bits"). Because values are fixed (so-called "discrete values"), digital data is more reliable than analog, as the latter is susceptible to sometimes uncontrollable physical variations.

digital watermark An invisible "marker" added to an image to identify it as the owner's property. (Details of watermarking software can be found at www.digimarc.com.)

digitize, **digitalize** To convert anything, such as text, images, or sound, into binary form so that it can be digitally processed, manipulated, stored, and reconstructed.

dither(ing) The term describing a technique of "interpolation" which calculates the average value of adjacent pixels. This technique is used either to add extra pixels to an image—to smooth an edge, for example, as in "antialiasing"—or to reduce the number of colors or grays in an image by replacing them with average values that conform to a predetermined palette of colors, such as when an image containing millions of colors is converted ("resampled") to a fixed palette ("index") of 256 colors—in Web use, for example. A color monitor operating in 8-bit color mode (256 colors) will automatically create a dithered pattern of pixels. Dithering is also used by some printing devices to simulate colors or tones.

DNS see domain name service

document The term describing the entire contents of a single HTML file. HTML documents are generally referred to as "web pages," since this is how they are rendered for display by browsers.

document heading An HTML style ("tag") which defines text headings in a range of predetermined sizes and weights (levels 1 through 6) so that you can add emphasis to a line of text.

document root The term describing the place on a Web server where all the HTML files,

images, and other components for a particular Web site are located.

document transfer rate The speed, measured in documents per minute, at which Web pages are transmitted to your computer once you have requested them.

domain name (**service**) (**DNS**) The description of a Web site's "address"—the means by which you find or identify a particular Web site, much like a brand name or trademark. A Web site address is actually a number which conforms to the numerical Internet protocol (IP) addresses that computers use for information exchange—but names are far easier for us to remember. Domain names are administered by the InterNIC organization and include at least two parts: the "subdomain," typically a company or organization; and the "high-level domain," which is the part after the first dot, such as in ".com" for commercial sites, ".org" for non-profit sites, ".gov" for governmental sites, ".edu" for educational sites, and so on. The high-level domain name may also indicate a country code for sites outside the United States (although a site without a country code does not necessarily mean it is inside the U.S.), such as ".uk" for the United Kingdom, ".de" for Germany, ".fr" for France, and so on.

doorway see home page

dpi Dots per inch. A unit of measurement used to represent the resolution of printers and imagesetters. The resolution of a monitor is often expressed in dpi.

DTD (abb.: Document Type Definition) A formal SGML specification for a document which lays out structural elements and markup definitions.

duotone Strictly speaking, a print term in which a monochromatic image is printed with different tonal ranges made from the same original so that, when printed in different tones of the same color (usually black, thus sometimes described as a "double-black duotone"), a wider tonal range is reproduced than is possible with a single color. The term is sometimes used erroneously to describe a "duplex halftone" or "false duotone" (a duplicate halftone printed in two colors).

dynamic HTML (**DHTML**) A recent version of HTML, with features tailored to Web innovations such as JavaScript applets. Web pages with a DHTML component will not work on browsers unable to interpret DHTML.

e-commerce Commercial transactions conducted electronically over a network or the Internet.

embedded object Hyperlinks, buttons, or rollovers set within the otherwise plain ASCII text of an HTML document.

external reference A resource that resides in a location outside of the application using it.

FAQ (abb.: frequently asked questions) A list, often posted on Web pages or in promotional literature, of answers to the most common questions asked by purchasers of software or hardware, or users of Internet services.

Flash (Macromedia) Software for creating vector graphics and animations for Web presentations. Flash generates small files which are correspondingly quick to download and, being vector, are scalable to any dimension without an increase in file size.

footer In an HTML document, the concluding part, containing information such as the date, version, etc.

form A term describing fillable spaces (fields) on a Web page which provide a means of collecting information and receiving feedback from people who visit a Web site. Forms can be used, for example, to buy an item, answer a questionnaire or access a database.

frame A way of breaking up a scrollable browser window on a Web page into several independent windows. Frames enable one to fix arbitrary sections of the available browser window space—e.g., a logo, a menu button bar, or an animation can be placed in one part of the browser window while another part is left available for information from a different Web page. Frames are available as several types. Basic frames feature a number of border types and color schemes and can be used to delineate screen areas. Borderless frames, a variation of the basic frame, make it possible to create aesthetically pleasing screens with separate fixed and scrolling

185

areas, without falling victim to the dreaded "through a keyhole" appearance. Floating or inline frames can be positioned anywhere in the browser window—unlike normal frames, which must always have at least one edge at the browser's window margin.

FTP (*abb.*: file transfer protocol) Standard protocol for file transfer across the Internet.

gateway A device or program used to connect disparate computer networks.

GIF (*abb.*: graphics interchange format) One of the main bitmapped image formats used on the Internet. Devised by Compuserve, an Internet Service Provider (now part of AOL), thus sometimes (although rarely) referred to as "Compuserve GIF," GIF (pronounced "jif") is a a 256-color format with two specifications, GIF87a and, more recently, GIF89a, the latter providing additional features such as transparent backgrounds. The GIF format uses a "lossless" compression technique, or "algorithm," and thus does not squeeze files as much as does the JPEG format, which is "lossy" (some data is discarded). For use in Web browsers, JPEG is the format of choice for tone images such as photographs, whereas GIF is more suitable for line images and other graphics such as text.

global Renaming software which updates all occurrences of a name throughout a Web site when one instance of that name is altered.

graphics interchange format see GIF

header file Files that contain information identifying incoming data transmitted via the Internet.

heading A formatting term used in HTML which determines the size at which text will be displayed in a WWW browser. There are six sizes, available usually referred to as H1, H2, H3, H4, H5, and H6.

helper application Applications which assist Web browsers in delivering or displaying information, such as movie or sound files.

hierarchical structure The term describing a technique of arranging information in a graded order which establishes priorities and therefore helps the user find a path that leads

them to what they want. Used extensively in networking and databases.

history (**list**) The term used to describe a list of visited Web pages which your browser logs during a session on the Web. The history provides a means of speedy access to pages already visited during that session.

hit counter A simple display on a Web page, resembling the mileage counter in a car, which provides a running count of the number of visitors to a site.

home page (index page, doorway) The main, introductory page on a Web site, usually with a title and tools to navigate through the rest of the site.

host A networked computer which provides services to anyone who can access it, such as for e-mail, file transfer, and access to the Web.

HotJava A Web browser, developed by Sun Microsystems, which is written in the Java programming language.

hotlist A theme-related list on a Web page which provides links to other pages or sites dedicated to that theme.

hotspot A clickable area in an image that contains an anchor or a hyperlink. *See also* image map.

HTML (*abb.*: HyperText Markup Language) A comparatively simple system of "tags" (HTML is not a programming language) that specify type styles and sizes, the location of graphics, and other information required to construct a Web page. To provide for increasingly complex presentations such as animation, sound, and video, the basic form of HTML is seeded with miniature computer programs, or applets, which are written using a scripting language. HTML documents include the essential instructions for publishing pages in cyberspace and are almost always accompanied by support files such as illustrations, buttons, animations, sounds, and video clips. A recent version, HTML 4.0, incorporates DHTML and supports cascading style sheets.

HTML table A grid on a Web page consisting of rows and columns of cells allowing precise positioning of text, pictures, movie clips, or any other element. A table can be nested

within another table. Tables offer a way of giving the appearance of multi-column layouts. They can be visible, with cells framed by borders, or invisible and used only to demarcate areas containing the elements on the page. A table is specified in terms of either a pixel count, which fixes its size irrespective of the browser or screen resolution used to view it, or as a percentage of the available screen space, allowing resizing to fit the browser window.

http (*abb.*: Hypertext Transfer Protocol) A text-based set of rules by which files on the World Wide Web are transferred, defining the commands that Web browsers use to communicate with Web servers. The vast majority of World Wide Web addresses, or "URLs," are prefixed with "http://."

https (*abb.*: hypertext transfer protocol secure) Synonymous with "http" but providing a secure link for such things as commercial transactions—on-line shopping with credit cards, for example—or access to password protected information.

hyperlink A contraction of "hypertext link," a clickable link to another location on the Web or within the same Web site. The hyperlink is the most basic and frequently used unit of a Web page. Anchor links allow navigation around a single Web page; clicking on the link scrolls the page to a specific point elsewhere on the same page. A button is a simple hyperlinked graphic—for example, the submit and reset buttons on interactive forms. Radio buttons allow users to select from a range of options. A rollover button changes in some way as the mouse pointer passes over it without anything having to be clicked. Typical rollovers are submit buttons, which are highlighted when the pointer passes over them, embedded links that darken to show that they are "live", and images of products that change to display a price. The text hyperlink is usually indicated by underlining and a highlight color, which often changes when the link has been invoked. A common example of a text hyperlink is the clickable URL.

hypermedia The combination of graphics, text, movies, sound, and other elements accessible via hypertext links in an on-line document or Web page.

hypertext A programming concept which links any single word or group of words to an unlimited number of others, typically text on a Web page which has an embedded link to other documents or Web sites. Hypertext links are usually underlined and/or in a different color to the rest of the text and are activated by clicking on them.

IETF (*abb.*: Internet Engineering Task Force) A suborganization of the Internet Architecture Board (IAB), comprising a group of volunteers that investigates and helps solve Internet-related problems and makes recommendations to appropriate Internet committees.

image map An image which contains a series of embedded links to other documents or Web sites. These links are activated when clicked on in the appropriate area of the image. For example, an image of a globe may incorporate an embedded link for each visible country which, when clicked, will take the user to a document giving more information about that country.

index page see home page

interlacing Downloading GIF images in alternate bands one pixel high. Bands 2, 4, 6, etc., are received before bands 1, 3, 5,_, allowing a full but incomplete image to be displayed after only half the data have been downloaded. Because of the way they are compressed, JPEG images cannot be interlaced, though a recent development of the format (progressive JPEG) produces a similar effect.

interleaved, interleaving The technique of displaying an image on screen—using a Web browser for example—so that it is revealed as a whole in increasing layers of detail rather than bit by bit from the top down. The image appears gradually, starting with slices which are eventually filled in when all the pixels appear.

intermediate code A representation of computer code which lies somewhere between code which can be read by you or I (such as HTML source code) and machine-readable binary code (1s and 0s). Java bytecode is one such example.

Internet A globe-spanning network of computer networks (INTERconnected NETwork) devised partly in response to a U.S. military need for a computer network able to survive a nuclear war.

ISP (*abb.*: Internet service provider) The surfer's gateway to the Internet. An ISP provides computers, known as servers, on which its customers' Web sites are stored, and may offer a range of other services.

Java A programming language devised for creating small applications ("applets") which can be downloaded from a Web server and used, typically in conjunction with a Web browser, to add dynamic effects such as animations.

JavaScript A "scripting" language which provides a simplified method of applying dynamic effects to Web pages.

JPEG (*abb.*: Joint Photographic Experts Group) A group that devised a file format—also called JPEG (pronounced "jay-peg")—for compressing bitmapped images. The degree of compression (from high compression/low-quality to low compression/high-quality) can be defined by the user, making the format doubly suitable for images which are to be used either for print reproduction or for transmitting over the Internet—for viewing in Web browsers, for example.

Kbps (*abb.*: kilobits per second) A measurement of the speed at which data is transferred across a network, a kilobit being 1,024 bits or characters.

knock back The process by which the intensity of a graphic is reduced (usually to render it suitable as a background image).

layout element The description of any component in the layout of an HTML document—a Web page, for example—such as a graphic, list, rule, paragraph, and so on.

link A pointer, such as a highlighted piece of text, in an HTML document (a Web page, for example) or multimedia presentation which takes the user to another location, page, or screen just by clicking on it.

list element Text in a Web page which is displayed as a list and which is defined by the HTML tag <LI> (list item).

list tag The name describing the HTML coding ("tags") which tells a Web browser how to display text in a variety of list styles, such as ordered lists <OL>, menus <MENU>, and glossary lists <DL>.

listserv An automated mailing list distribution system, typically based on UNIX servers.

logical style Browser-specific style for HTML text, such as "emphasis" or "strong." How these styles are displayed depends on the visitor's browser. *See also* physical style *and* preformatted style.

Lynx A text-only browser that does not display or load images.

markup The technique of embedding "tags" (HTML instructions) within special characters ("metacharacters") which tell a program such as a Web browser how to display a page.

markup language A defined set of rules for describing the way files are displayed by any particular method. HTML is one such language, used for creating Web pages.

marquee see ticker-tape streamer

master page The opening or index page of a Web site from which further sub-pages are linked.

Mbps (*abb.*: megabits per second) A measure of data transfer speeds.

metacharacter Characters within text which indicate formatting, such as the "tags" in an HTML file. Angle brackets (< >) and ampersands (&) are typical metacharacters.

MIDI Sound file format for synthesizers playable by PC and Mac browsers.

Mosaic The first Web browser with a graphical, point-and-click interface, written by Marc Andreessen in 1992 after discovering Tim Berners-Lee's World Wide Web. Initially developed for the Unix and Linux operating systems, Mosaic's transition to the PC and Apple Mac attracted a million users to the Web within just one year.

MPEG (*abb.*: Moving Picture Experts Group) A working group of ISO/IEC in charge of the development of standards for the coded representation of digital audio and video. Established in 1988, the group produced MPEG-1, the standard on which video CD and MP3

187

are based; MPEG-2, the standard on which digital television set-top boxes and DVD are based; and MPEG-4, the standard for multimedia on the Web. The current thrust is MPEG-7, "Multimedia Content Description Interface." Work on the new standard MPEG-21, "Multimedia Framework," started in June 2000.

multimedia General term referring to the use of sound, graphics, video, and other features—often in interactive form—in computer-based applications, including the Web.

navigate The process of finding your way around a multimedia presentation or Web site by clicking on words or buttons.

navigation bar A special bar in a Web browser, Web page, or multimedia presentation which helps you to "navigate" through pages by clicking on buttons or text.

navigation button A button in a Web browser, Web page, or multimedia presentation which links you to a particular location or page.

on-line Any activity taking place on a computer or device while it is connected to a network such as the Internet. The opposite of off-line.

orphan file A file on a Web site which is not referred to by any link or button and thus cannot be reached by any means other than through its absolute URL—in other words, to find it you must know its exact pathname.

page An HTML document (text structured with HTML tags) viewed with a Web browser.

pane see frame

paragraph In an HTML document, a markup tag <P> used to define a new paragraph in text.

PDF (*abb.*: portable document format)

PFR see Truedoc

Physical style HTML Text style, such as italic or bold, that is displayed in much the same way by all browsers. See also logical style and preformatted style.

Plug-in Subsidiary software for a browser or other package that enables it to perform additional functions, e.g., play sound, movies, or video.

PNG (*abb.*: portable network graphics) A new digital image format using a highly sophisticated compression technique that is said to result in file sizes typically 30 percent smaller than those for comparable GIFs.

Portable font resources (**PFR**) see Truedoc

Portable network graphics see PNG

Preformatted style HTML Text style, denoted by <PRE> tags, that uses a monospaced font such as Courier to reproduce text exactly as it is imported into the Web document. This is useful for rendering computer code and other text where exact reproduction is required. See also logical style and physical style.

QuickTime Computer movie software developed by Apple, but now also in use on PCs.

RealAudio (RealNetworks) Software for streaming audio.

request The term describing the act of clicking on a button or link in a Web browser—in fact, making a request to a remote server for an HTML document.

resolution, monitor resolution, screen resolution The number of pixels a screen can display, expressed as pixels across by pixels down. The three most common resolutions are 640x480, 800x600, and 1024x768. The current standard Web page size is 800x600.

RMF (*abb.*: rich music format) A less common sound file format.

script, scripting language Computer programming languages used to write applets, which provide the more sophisticated features seen on modern Web pages. Examples are Netscape's JavaScript and Microsoft's Jscript and VBscript.

scripting tag see tag

search engine The part of a program (such as a database) which seeks out information in response to requests made by the user. On the Web, search engines such as Yahoo, HotBot, and Alta Vista provide sophisticated criteria for searching, summaries of each result, and the Web site addresses for retrieving more information.

search tool A program which enables specific Web pages to be searchable.

secure area The part of a Web site where personal or sensitive information can be filled in by users. Secure areas are usually identified by the prefix "https" in the URL and are particularly important for commercial transactions made via the Web.

secure server A computer maintained by an ISP that processes sensitive data, such as credit card details, which Web users might not want to send by ordinary e-mail.

server Computer run by an ISP that provides access to the Internet for the ISP's customers.

Shocked The term applied to Web pages that contain material prepared with Macromedia's Shockwave technology, and thus require the Shockwave plug-in in order to be viewed.

Shockwave A technology developed by Macromedia for creating Director presentations which can be delivered across the Internet and viewed with a Web browser.

singleton An HTML "tag" without a corresponding closing tag.

streaming video/audio A method of transmitting video or audio that allows it to be played continuously and apparently in real time. Segments of the received data are buffered while the user's video/audio software plays the previously buffered section.

style sheet Enables designers to set up a style and apply it to text in one easy action.

syntax The arrangement of words, showing their grammatical relationship. In programming languages such as those used for creating multimedia presentations and HTML documents for the Web, syntax describes the correct use of the programming according to a given set of rules.

syntax checker A program which checks a programmer's use of a particular programming language against the rules set for that language.

tag, text tag, tag pair In HTML, simple code or instructions placed between <> characters to instruct a browser to display text in a particular style. The tags are always placed in pairs, one at the beginning and the other at the end of the text to be styled.

teaser A link on a Web page designed to tempt visitors into clicking further into the site.

tenant People who administrate a Web site located on another person's server, typically one belonging to an Internet Service Provider (ISP).

terminal emulation Software which allows your computer to mimic another, remote, computer by acting as a terminal for the other—in other words, it is as though you are actually working on that remote computer.

text hyperlink see hyperlink

text mode see character mode

thumbnail A small version of a larger image, to which it is linked. When the visitor clicks the thumbnail, the larger image is downloaded and displayed, sometimes in a new window.

ticker-tape streamer A horizontally scrolling line of text which is used to catch the attention and provide information that would be dull if it were static. Currently popular on Web sites.

tile An image repeated two or more times to create a background. A background image, smaller than the size of the screen (which is, in turn, arbitrary), is automatically tiled to fill the screen.

title In a Web page, text which appears on that page's title bar.

transparency Allows a GIF image to be blended into the background by ridding it of unwanted background color.

Truedoc System used by the type manufacturer Bitstream to transmit an image of the fonts used in a Web page so that they display accurately at the destination. The system uses a browser plug-in along with portable font resources (PFR). Such fonts cannot be used in other applications on the visitor's machine.

UNIX An operating system developed by AT&T, devised to be multitasking and portable from one machine to another. UNIX is used widely on Web servers.

URI (abb.: Uniform Resource Identifier) Something which identifies resources available to the Web, such as a URL.

URL (abb.: Uniform Resource Locator) The unique address of a page on the Web, comprising three elements: the protocol to be used (such as http), the domain name ("host"), and the directory name followed by pathnames to any particular file.

URL-encoded text A method of encoding text for passing requests from your Web browser to a server.

URN (abb.: Uniform Resource Name) A permanent name for a Web resource.

USB (abb.: Universal Serial Bus) A port (socket) for connecting peripheral devices to your computer which can be daisy-chained together. These can include devices such as scanners, printers, keyboards, and hard drives.

Usenet Acronym for user's network, in which a vast number of articles, categorized into newsgroups, are posted by individuals on every conceivable subject. These are hosted on servers throughout the world in which you can post your own articles to people who subscribe to those newsgroups. Special "newsreader" software is required to view the articles.

virtual shopping cart A method of providing Web shoppers with a means of selecting items for purchase as they browse a site, paying for them all at once when done—just as you would in any store.

VRML (abb.: Virtual Reality Modeling Language) An HTML-type programming language designed to create 3D scenes called "virtual worlds."

W3 see World Wide Web

W3C see World Wide Web Consortium

WAIS (abb.: Wide Area Information Service) A system developed to access information in indexed databases across the Internet.

watermark The technique of applying a tiled graphic to the background of a Web page, which remains fixed, no matter what foreground materials scroll across it.

.wav File name extension for "wave" format sound files. Wave files originate in the PC world but also work with Apple Mac browsers.

Web see World Wide Web

WebEdit Pro (Nesbitt Software) HTML editor.

Web master The person responsible for a Web site (usually spelled Webmaster).

Web page A published HTML document on the World Wide Web.

Web server A computer (host) dedicated to Web services.

Web site The address, location (on a server), and collection of documents and resources for any particular interlinked set of Web pages.

WEFT (abb.: Web embedding font tool) Microsoft's solution to the problem of downloading fonts without breach of copyright. WEFT offers four levels of licensing, which range from fonts that can be freely installed on the visitor's computer to fonts that are restricted to display within the browser. WEFT does not require a plug-in. See also Truedoc.

World Wide Web (abb.: WWW) The network of sites hosted on computers (usually dedicated servers) throughout the world and navigable by hyperlinks. The Web was originally conceived by Tim Berners-Lee, a programmer at CERN, who sought to link, or cross-reference, the information on the Internet, a backup communications system set up by the U.S. military. Interest in the Web was considerably increased when Marc Andreessen developed the first Web browser with a graphical interface, Mosaic, for Unix and Linux operating systems and then ported it for use on PCs and Apple machines. The Web should be distinguished from the Internet, which is a more inclusive term.

World Wide Web Consortium (abb.: W3C) The organization which is jointly responsible with the IETF for maintaining and managing standards across the Web.

X Windows A GUI used on UNIX computers.

X-face An encoded 48 × 48 bitmap image used by e-mail and news users to contain a picture of their face or company logo.

Xobject External objects, such as sounds and movies, which are used in Macromedia Director presentations.

189

INDEX

URLs

www.abbeynational.co.uk 74
www.absolut.com 171
www.actionman.com 142
www.airfrance.com 124
www.alessi.com 152, 153
www.apple.com 96, 97
www.arnolfini.demon.co.uk 94
www.artfuldog.com 140
www.artnet.com 100–1
www.att.com 114, 115
www.audi.com 174, 175
www.audi.de 63
www.bauhaus.de 102
www.bbc.co.uk 118–19
www.bedbathandbeyond.com 146
www.beetle.de/newversion.htm 86
www.benandjerrys.com 138
www.benetton.com 130
www.bigbrother.com 162
www.blaupunkt.de 152
www.bmwgroup.com 102, 103
www.bol.com 147
www.buckinfudgy.com 71
www.carandache.ch 168
www.caravan.com 163
www.cartier.fr 166
www.citroen.com 36, 69
www.cnn.com 116, 117
www.cocacola.com 84
www.conran.co.uk 88–9
www.cyberlive.com 71
www.daler-rowney.com 168, 169
www.damienhirst.co.uk 36
www.deltavacations.com 125
www.designmuseum.org 126, 127
www.diesel.com 148–9
www.digimarc.com 61
www.discovery.com 119
www.dixons.com 68
www.dkny.com 10
www.drmartens.com 158
www.dwelle.de 116
www.dyson.co.uk 152
www.eckhart.nl 72
www.egg.com 74, 164–5
www.elle.com 172
www.ericsson.com 114
www.fuse98.com 32–3
www.goldfish.com 112, 113
www.greenpeace.org 39
www.guardian.com 120, 121

www.gucci.it 166
www.guinness.ie 170–1
www.habitat.net 90–1
www.heineken.com 171
www.hmv.com 63
www.ikea.com 122–3
www.inspop.com 166
www.intel.com 132–3
www.iomega.com 96
www.jeepunpaved.com 106
www.jthin.co.uk 73
www.kelloggs.com 75
www.kitsch.co.uk 37
www.kodak.com 57, 70–1
www.lego.com 154
www.levi.com 84
www.louvre.fr 105
www.marbles.com 112
www.mastercard.com 112–3
www.melinamade.com 62, 160
www.memphismagazine.com 120
www.metadesign.com 10
www.milk.co.uk 170
www.modernauction.com 57
www.moma.org 108, 109
www.mothkettle.com 69
www.motown.com 129
www.natwest.com 136
www.nescafe.com 73, 138, 139
www.nextdada.luc.ac.be 94
www.nissan.com 106, 107
www.npower.com 110
www.oshkoshbgosh.com 146
www.paulsmith.co.uk 68, 156–7
www.peapod.com 144
www.pentagram.com 179
www.playmobil.com 154, 155
www.prophetcomm.com 36
www.realaudio.com 79
www.realnetworks.com 79
www.retroactive.com 160
www.revlon.com 134, 135
www.rijksmuseum.nl 126
www.saatchila.com 178
www.sainsbury.co.uk 144
www.sfmoma.org 104–5
www.shoplink.com 144
www.sirius.com 75
www.smeg.nl 17
www.snackums.com 92
www.sony.com 128

www.sparkasse.de 137
www.supersoaker.com 142, 143
www.teleport.com 134
www.tesco.com 144, 145
www.the-body-shop.com 98–9
www.thesunglasscity.com 157
www.thumb.co.uk 17
www.tiffany.com 166
www.tigertoys.com/poochi 141
www.tivola.de 138
www.tpd.co.uk 37
www.uboc.com 136
www.ubs.com 137
www.ucla.edu 62
www.umax.com 176
www.usatoday.com 120
www.virgin.com 128, 129
www.vizability.com 10
www.vogue.com 172–3
www.volvo.com 174
www.webspice.com 29
www.wineskinny.com 120
www.women.nikejapan.co.jp 82
www.yamaha.com 152
www.yellowpages.co.uk 56
www.zanussi.com 177
www.zippo.com 17, 108